Where IS Your Mother?

A Simple and Suggestive Guide to Basic Etiquette and Simple Grace

AVA CARROLL-BROWN

iUniverse, Inc.
Bloomington

Where IS Your Mother?
A Simple and Suggestive Guide to Basic Etiquette and Simple Grace

iUniverse books may be ordered through booksellers or by contacting:

iUniverse
1663 Liberty Drive
Bloomington, IN 47403
www.iuniverse.com
1-800-Authors (1-800-288-4677)

ISBN: 978-1-4620-0954-1 (sc)
ISBN: 978-1-4620-0955-8 (hc)
ISBN: 978-1-4620-0956-5 (e)

Printed in the United States of America

Library of Congress Control Number: 2011907503

iUniverse rev. date: 6/8/2011

Contents

Dedication

Since the beginning of time, a mother, or mother-like figure has been the teacher, the nurse, the protector, and the ever-strong glue of the family structure. Think about this:

When a child at play gets hurt, the question will ring, "Where is your mother?"

When a toddler chooses to act out, the question is asked, "Where is your mother?"

And when a family member displays less than desirable manners or behavior, the question is always presented, "Where is your mother?"

In answer to all of these questions, I dedicate this book on basic etiquette and simple grace, and in honor of the ever present and my favorite question of...

"Where is your mother?"

To every person from the age of two to one hundred.

To my incredible husband who has endured many years of that look from across the table, yet has continued to encourage me to put pen to paper and share with others the basics of my experiences, knowledge, and observations.

To my wonderful and successful, now-grown children, in appreciation of all the rules they were required to follow; all of the handmade thank you cards they were encouraged to make and the many conversations that they were forced to endure even though they were not invited to participate in. And to their spouses, who are now part of the family and expected to follow suit.

To my adorable grandchildren, while enjoying sushi in our favorite restaurant, strapped in a high chair to ensure control of their behavior; for our ever-famous family rule that has been passed down from generation to generation, regarding a no-thank-you helping; which mandates at least a small serving of whatever has been prepared, like it or not; and for the many kisses that continue to be placed all over their faces, no matter where we are or who may be watching.

And most importantly in hopes of awakening the lessons on basic etiquette and simple grace that were once the past, are now the present, and will forever be part of the future, and for the answer to the lifelong question, *"Where IS your mother?"*

Preface

After many years in the event production industry, it has become a surprising realization that socially, the majority of people, young and old alike, do not have the slightest idea about proper etiquette and social grace. The reference books from long ago, written by the etiquette experts, remain on the shelves at bookstores, failing to reach the homes of the families of today. Many say that proper etiquette and good manners are things of the past and not important any longer, believing that in this world of high tech and international ventures, anything goes. I am a strong supporter of the other group; the group that is completely—and will be forever—convinced that proper etiquette and social grace are the foundation of that very important first impression that we all make every day of our lives, and I believe these ideals are here to stay.

Proper etiquette is based on common sense and, in a given situation, is followed because it is the proper thing to do. Social etiquette, or grace, is based on the rules and guidelines outlined by experts such as Emily Post and Amy Vanderbilt, and is the socially expected thing to do. None of these practices will ever go out of style. They are the finishing touches of every well-groomed individual, personal and professional, and should be included on their long list of qualities. We are not born with good manners or social grace, but we have all been made aware of their importance during our lives. We all simply need to be reminded of that importance, at one time or another during our lives, and with that knowledge, we can conquer the highest mountain and achieve the most amazing dreams.

We are all reminded of the basics as we partake in the sport of "people watching," observing people in our neighborhood, at school, or at work. Whether it be at the mall, or waiting on a bench for public transportation, walking in an amusement park, cheering from the bleachers in a sports arena, or just sitting in a car waiting for a light to change, the sport of people watching will captivate us all from one time or another—and, oh, the stories we could tell. On occasion, we are enlightened, as we can learn from the actions we see. And other times we are left with questions, as we observe a less-than-acceptable behavior presented right before our eyes.

One of my favorite locations to really get involved in this amusing and entertaining people sport is at any social event. A wedding, an awards dinner, a birthday—whether it be social, corporate, or a Hollywood studio event—the combination of the people, their habits, their presentation of manners, or lack thereof, creates great entertainment and is the inspiration for this book.

We have all heard the questions, "Wouldn't it be wonderful ... if there was a book for raising the perfect children ... if there was a manual for obtaining the perfect job ... if there was a guide for finding the perfect mate?"

Quite possibly, the answers to those questions can be answered by the guidance from a parent, direction from a mentor, or teaching from a teacher—even the basics of proper etiquette and simple grace.

This book has been created to serve as a fast and friendly reference for answers to many of the questions relating to the basics of proper etiquette and simple grace. For young or old, and any age in between, the basic steps of proper etiquette and good manners will unfold in the pages to follow.

Who Am I to Say?

Beginning as a toddler, into the Kindergarten classroom and onto our retirement years, which hopefully will be enjoyed on a perfectly manicured golf course or sailing around the world on our own private yacht, questions of basic etiquette and social grace seem to surface on a daily basis.

When do we write a thank you note?

When is it proper to give a gift?

What do we do with our napkin?

Why do we need all that silverware?

This book has been created to answer many of the basic day-to-day etiquette questions, simply and clearly, and to encourage the importance of remembering the etiquette rules established by experts such as Post and Vanderbilt many years ago. When in doubt, refer to old world proper etiquette.

These are the same simple rules that were taught to us by our parents and our grandparents throughout our lives, and hopefully, are the same rules that we will teach to our children, encouraging their practice on a daily basis.

For whatever reason, the greater population of today's world seems to feel that proper etiquette and good manners are things of the past. Well, I am here to state that proper etiquette and good manners are here to stay and are the core of our meaning. The first impression that you make in any situation will last a lifetime, and simple grace, hand-in-hand with good manners, will be the introduction to your life story. It is true that class cannot be purchased, nor etiquette for that matter, and it is highly doubtful that social status can be offered through a store or on a website; however, we can all learn the tools of basic etiquette and social grace to assist in making who we are, the best that we can be.

Where IS Your Mother? is written for today's world, for today's people, from toddlers to the elderly, and for today's situations. Simple etiquette and proper social grace are like the perfect invitation—visible and meaningful—and are the first impressions of who we are or ever hope to become.

Simple etiquette, outlined by the experts over the years, and proper social grace, based on common sense and the proper thing to do, will open doors and provide each and every one of us a sound and confident position in any direction that we may choose to take and prepare us for what may lay ahead.

So sit back and enjoy as the story unfolds before you. Stories that are simple and fun to read, but most importantly, are filled with sound common sense, easy-to-apply suggestions, and the basic rules on the subjects of etiquette, good manners, and proper social grace. Each chapter will outline the basic points of etiquette and protocol from years past and for the years to follow; an enjoyable feast of information filled with suggestions that we all can enjoy from the incredible and proper banquet of simple grace.

Chapter One

So, This Is the Table

WE ALL HAVE stories about our experiences while at the table. Those "Kodak" moments when elbows are used as swords guarding the food in front of us, elbow-and-hand braces are used as a pedestal to hold up our heavy heads, or legs stretched out and crossed, placed parallel to the table extending into the walking area, creating an obstacle course for anyone who may venture to serve or even walk by. There are also the sleepers, those who obviously are too tired to even be at the table, head-in-hand, slumping into their plates, and sometimes even laying their head down as if the table were a pillow.

How enjoyable for us all, especially for those who have taken the time to prepare a lovely meal and are rewarded by looking at a sleepy, slumped-over, human obstacle course. Possibly, it would have been a better idea to just place a pet dish on the floor so the food could be gulped down at the guest's leisure; or maybe, instead of a dinner invitation, an invitation should have been extended to just come over and lounge on the sofa and not bother to be seated at the table at all. I don't think so!

I am a firm believer that there is a time and a place for everything. When at a dining table, it is the time and place to eat: sitting upright in your chair, legs tucked underneath the table, and feet placed firmly on the floor or in that direction. The purpose of your hands is to hold and operate eating utensils, not to support or hold up your head. Elbows are the usable extensions of the hand-to-mouth motion, to be kept off the table at all times and placed close to your sides.

Your meal space at a dining table is measured by the width of your chair seat, continuing to the immediate left and right of your place setting.

1

No need to place those elbows on the table for support or to balance your fork and knife; your eating utensils will never become that heavy.

No need to use those elbows as a weapon to guard your meal space; they will be just fine at your sides and, surprisingly, that is exactly where they were intended to be kept.

And definitely no improper sitting at the table; your chair should be placed square to the edge of the table. Sit tall on the seat of your chair. Tuck your legs underneath the table with your feet on the floor or in that direction.

No sitting on your legs; legs were not intended to be a booster chair. If you need a little boost to be closer to the table, a proper chair can be purchased at numerous locations, often for a very reasonable price. If dining outside of your home, booster chairs are available upon request.

No walking around your chair; the dining table is not an athletic track or park. When the meal has been completed, excuse yourself from the table and walk wherever you wish, away from the dining table, and during the meal, remain seated.

And no squirming around like a restless animal. When you are invited to sit at the table, the assumption is that you are human, so act accordingly. Sit and enjoy the meal that has been placed in front of you.

The list of items that can be covered under this topic could go on forever, and we will only begin to scratch the surface of a few of the more important lessons in basic etiquette and good manners.

This chapter has been divided into several important sections, presented simply and clearly, so sit and enjoy the information, and when you have completed this chapter, you will be able to indulge in a banquet of knowledge and each feasting table will be your oyster.

Fact: The reason a table with chairs placed around it is called a dining table is for the purpose of people to come together, to be seated, and to dine.

Secondary purposes for a dining table may include a surface on which to do homework, a table for art projects or sewing, or even a space for board games.

But at least once a day, it is strongly suggested that in every home the table be used as intended—to sit at properly to dine.

Wouldn't it be wonderful if the entire family could come together at the same time and for the same reason? What an exciting concept! The most convenient time to plan this gathering would be dinnertime. Parent(s) have returned home from a long day at work, the kids have hopefully completed their homework and art projects, and hobbies have been put away for the evening. The music lessons and sports practices are finished for the night; it is the end of a long and full day, and everyone is hungry! And at the end of each day, there is much to talk about, so inviting the entire family to come together to sit around the dining table and share a meal is a natural and productive thing to do. It is the perfect opportunity for conversation, to get to know what everyone else is doing and, most importantly, to enjoy time together as a family, getting back to the basics and returning to the family unit.

When I was growing up, most mothers were homemakers—not anymore. Today, in many families, both parents are working and the kids have their studies, lessons, a social life, and sports. And believe it or not, many kids still are expected to do chores around the house. You remember: little jobs like mowing the lawn or dusting and vacuuming the family room. But family, no matter how large or small or how many projects its members are involved in during the course of the day, family remains family, and that fact will never change.

In this very busy world, a table is seldom used for its main purpose, and that purpose is coming together as a family to dine. Everyone is always in a hurry, partaking of meals on the way out the door, in their bedrooms, in front of the TV, and even while on the telephone; everywhere but at the dining table. Ask yourself this question, "How long does it take to share a meal?"

Answer? Probably less than thirty minutes or maybe an hour; but during that time, as a parent, you have the opportunity to talk to your children and actually get to know who they are, who their friends are, and what they are doing with their time away from home and during the day. As a child, you have the perfect opportunity of sharing who you are with your family, letting them know what excites you, your feelings and your dreams, and creating and maintaining an important open line of communication with your parents and siblings. An open line of communication is a very special key that needs to be established in every household between the children and the parents.

Agreed, everyone is busy; but everyone needs to eat as well, correct? We should take time, no, we *must* make time, at least once a day, to come together as a family, and the best meeting place in any household is the dining table.

Many years ago, my sister-in-law gave me a framed sign that still hangs proudly on my kitchen wall in view of anyone who sits at our table. It reads, "Anything that takes me more than two hours to cook should take you more than two minutes to eat."

When we come together at the dining table to share a meal, we should take the time to enjoy the meal and the opportunity to be with the family. Now relax and take a deep breath, as I am not suggesting that each night we all take two hours to prepare a meal; we all can agree that in the average household, we don't have two hours to prepare a meal every evening. But dinner has to be prepared, so take full advantage of the time.

Preparation time is also a great time to chat with your family, play catch-up on the daily news, and share time together—perhaps, on a one-on-one basis. Now, hold this thought: Time with your family is precious and valuable time that can never be replaced.

It is a time when everyone can be reminded just how special family really is, and it is an ideal opportunity to practice simple grace and apply basic table manners.

As parents, we can begin to teach the basic rules of simple grace and table manners before our children are two years old, and these practices can be continued throughout their lifetime with just a little day-to-day encouragement. Good manners are essential and are not a passing fancy. When using good manners, they will be appreciated by every person we encounter throughout our lives, personally and professionally, and when good manners are not present, that too will be noticed, but in a less desirable light. Naturally, the table manners of a two-year-old will not be perfect. However, they can certainly be encouraged each and every day; consistency is the foundation of any good learning technique. As your child grows, all of your efforts will be recognized and appreciated by your child as well as those around him or her. Of course, there are no guarantees that when your children are out by themselves in the world, they will behave like perfect little ladies and gentlemen. However, we all have that built-in recorder in our minds that seems to turn on when triggered by the slightest memory of any lesson, and the basics of good table manners, taught at an early age and encouraged throughout the years, will be one of those lessons. When these lessons are displayed, in the comfort of your own home or somewhere outside your home, they will be the parental guarantees that when triggered, will keep going and going, like the Energizer bunny, even in your absence.

The key point of this lesson is that the dining table is by definition, a space where family and friends come together, to share a meal, discuss the events of the day, and bond through conversation. This seems quite clear in statement; however, apparently it is not understood by most of today's population, young and old alike. So, once again, when one is sitting at a table, it means precisely—sit! No climbing, no walking around, no jumping, and no squirming; to sit means to sit. Very clear, agreed? There are rules in life wherever we go that offer guidelines and directions, and proper etiquette at the table is one of those rules.

Chapter Two

What About the Children?

HAVE YOU EVER been at a restaurant, family style or for a romantic getaway, or at the home of a friend, and a child begins jumping up and down on the seat behind you or at the table next to you, dropping unidentifiable objects in your hair, and eventually dumping the contents of an action character sippy cup down your back? How refreshing!

Or how about when you are sitting in a restaurant trying to enjoy a nice meal, when out of nowhere screams and tantrums, or an apparent meltdown, loud giggles, or whining from a child completely out of control, shatters the silence of your space like a box of firecrackers exploding on the fourth of July. How pleasant!

And of course, how about the children who are allowed to run up and down the service pathways, in between the guest dining tables, creating near-miss collisions with the unfortunate wait staff who are working so hard to please the entire room, still wearing big smiles as they protect the heavy tray of food they are carrying in fear of dropping it on top of the heads of the precious little pumpkins scrambling beneath them. How exciting!

I have even witnessed children standing or jumping on the actual dining table, as their parents sit in their own little world, completely oblivious to the sounds and actions of the bad behavior around them, continuing a conversation with whomever will listen, as if all was just perfect. Wake up!

Fact: This display of bad behavior by a child is not cute, nor is it appreciated by anyone around. The fact is, these acts of bad manners and obvious lack of parental control are not only annoying, but are potential liability issues for the parents and the proprietor of the establishment, as well as to the guests sitting in the dining space around the disturbance, and it is totally unacceptable for any parent to assume otherwise.

"Kids will be kids" is never an excuse for out-of-control children. What a dumb and inappropriate statement, and what does it actually mean? It makes about as much sense as the proprietor of a restaurant posting a sign that reads: "Although you have never visited our restaurant in the past, all items served will be perfect, and everything is free!"

I will agree that "kids *are* kids" and the interpretation of this statement is again, precisely, kids *are* kids, not wild animals, and should be taught to act accordingly.

As a parent or a supervising adult, to be so deeply hidden in the dark as to allow yourself to assume that bad behavior is as adorable to everyone around as it is to the parents who are permitting it to happen, is a big assumption! If this statement is questioned, just take a look around when your child is totally out of control—do you see any smiling faces? I don't think so. The reactions and expressions on the faces of those people seated around you, including other families with kids, will quickly confirm that when your child is behaving badly and your choice as a parent is to not take control of the situation, obviously in a delusional cloud of mistaken thinking, you will quickly be reminded that you and your belief stand alone! Harsh, but very true! To assume that a child can be placed in an adult situation and be expected to act like an adult is ridiculous! If this were a true assumption, all children would be born with angel wings, blessed with perfect manners, would have the vocabulary of a thirty-year-old, and the attention span of a college graduate, leaving no need for parents to guide, teach, and direct them.

Kids *are* kids!

As the parent, it is up to you to ensure that when your child is at the dining table, at home, or outside of the home, that this dining time is a pleasurable experience for everyone and that your child is kept completely under control—your control. When toddlers and small children are taken out for a meal, depending on their age and size, they should be placed in a highchair, booster chair, or be seated next to a parent or supervising adult throughout the entire meal. The child should be taught that at the table, he or she must remain seated! As adults, we are not permitted to wander around, to scream and yell, to toss our food, or behave inappropriately; we are expected to sit down and remain seated for the duration of the meal, unless of course, nature calls. This at-the-table rule is a given and begins at home for children as well as for adults. We are all products of our environment, so if good manners and proper table behavior are practiced at home, it only stands to reason that the good manners and proper behavior will be displayed outside of the comforts of home.

There are restaurants designed especially for kids and there are also restaurants that offer a kid's menu. These options offer a choice of foods that are enjoyable and easy to handle for small children, which makes your life easier. When taking your child out for a meal, and you are not certain if there is a menu designed for your little one, it only takes a moment to pick up the telephone and confirm if the restaurant you are visiting is child-friendly. If this is not the case, you as a parent, have a decision to make. Select another restaurant, or feed your child before you depart for the restaurant. You also have the option of bringing items that your child can eat.

Always remember that child-friendly does not just imply that there will be menu selections suitable for little ones. Child-friendly may also imply that if your child does escape from your supervision, the surroundings of the restaurant are child-safe and that the clientele is conducive to children. One must also be aware that there are restaurants suggested for adults only. Before you walk in the doors to any restaurant, it is always a good idea to confirm that the restaurant of your choice is indeed child-friendly. There are many restaurants that also offer kids' activity packages or items to assist in keeping a child happy and busy during the course of a meal. Crayons, coloring books or mats, or quiet games, are all items that kids enjoy and that can be played with at the table to assist in the control of proper behavior while having a meal outside of home; however, there is no guarantee that these items will work for the duration of the meal. You, as a parent, are the only one who can predict the turnout of your child's behavior, so always be prepared. Sometimes these activities help for a short period of time, but for whatever reason, they may not do the trick for the entire meal. Kids have a very short attention span and become bored easily. You know your children well enough to be able to determine what works and what does not. As a parent, one cannot always count on these items being available at every restaurant, so be prepared by placing a small ziplock bag of crayons, coloring pencils, and materials to draw on and pop the bag into your purse—a safety precaution that is highly recommended. A few small books may assist in quiet and proper behavior of the child while away from home; whatever it takes, be prepared. You are the parent and as the parent, it is your responsibility to keep the situation under control. It is not the responsibility of the restaurant or the guests in the restaurant to sit quietly and accept the fact that your kid is totally out of control!

Things happen, and even when we feel, as parents, that we are totally prepared for any situation, there are no guarantees that children will behave at a restaurant or anywhere else for that matter. But as a parent, we can teach our children proper and acceptable behavior that will carry through their adult life; they all begin with manners—good and proper manners.

It is suggested that when we bring our children into an adult situation, we follow a few simple rules that will assist in making the time away from the comfort of home a pleasant time for everyone: our children, ourselves, and those around us, perhaps welcoming a second visit.

Here are a few simple suggestions that can be followed when going out for a meal with a child:

1. Make sure that before you walk out of the door of your home that your child is happy. If your child is not feeling well, has missed a nap, if it is close to bedtime, or if he or she has simply had one of those "off" days, stay home or call a sitter. Taking a tired, ill, or unhappy child out for an evening is an invitation to a disaster.

2. Never assume that if your meal plans exceed past the child's usual mealtime that your child will be just fine until the meal is actually served. Your assumption will most certainly be incorrect. Remember the expression "egg on your face?" If you are insisting that your child has dinner at the same time that your dinner is served, give the child a snack before you leave for the evening. Your child, at any age, will be more content with just a few goldfish crackers or a container of crunchy cereal, which will hold him or her over until dinner is served, and everyone around you will thank you for the courtesy. If you assume otherwise, that is what is referred to as "egg on your face."

3. Never assume that the restaurant will have kids' items for children to play with while waiting for your order to be served to the table. Be safe and bring activities for your little ones. Crayons, activity books, coloring books, quiet hand games, or other items will keep little fingers busy and little ones happy in an adult situation.

4. Be aware of timing. This is a double-sided suggestion. No matter how old or well-behaved your child is, it if is past his or her bedtime, he or she should be home, tucked safely in his or her own bed, and certainly not forced to stay awake with the adults and be expected to act like a grownup. If you make the dinner reservations early, the clientele that will be seated around you will probably also have children and the out-of-home dinner experience will be more enjoyable for all concerned.

It really is unreasonable and ridiculous to place children in an adult situation and expect them to act like adults—that just doesn't happen! There are no guarantees that adults will act like adults in many situations, so in good sense, how can we expect our little ones to do so? But as parents, we do have the ability to somewhat control the situation by implicating a few safety measures, which, when applied, will encourage a pleasant outing using the tools of good common sense.

When your child is served a meal, at home or away from home, again, the common sense rule comes into play.

First, the child remains seated and is expected to eat the meal placed before him or her. No jumping, no standing, no squirming, and no wandering around. And especially no playing or tossing food while at the dining table.

If the child has already had their meal at home, the child is still expected to remain seated, doing the busy things that little people can do. Little projects, such as coloring, or puzzles, that will keep little hands busy, and grownups happy.

If your child is acting out, tired, or just upset, and cannot be consoled or quieted within a reasonable few moments, be considerate of those around you and take the child out of the restaurant until quiet time is achieved.

Most people really do love children, especially children that are well behaved. These few suggestions will assist you in teaching your child respect while in a public place and proper behavior at any dinner table. Acting out, temper tantrums, playing in their food, or tossing their meal across the table should never be allowed at home, nor should it be permitted outside of the home. The dining table is a place to be seated properly, to engage in a meal appropriately, and to act accordingly throughout the meal, no matter how old you are. If the games begin, and you as a parent do not or will not take the situation under control, it is time to be excused from the table. And when away from home, if you as a parent cannot or will not take control of the situation, the dinner must be declared over!

As a teenager or as an adult, good table manners must also apply. This is not a rule that is learned as a child and then forgotten. It is a proper etiquette rule that as children, we are taught and we conquer, and as we grow older, these good manners will naturally become a part of each and every day throughout our lives and automatically be applied at each and every meal we consume. Loud voices, leaning over, or on the table, shoveling food into your mouth, or graciously sharing bits of your meal while talking or chewing with your mouth open, are equally as unacceptable at any age. Sometimes just a look or a comment from a parent or an onlooker of the situation can trigger the recorder in your mind that holds the lessons on good table manners. And if you have been taught the basics of good table manners as a child, the recorder will kick in and will keep going and going and going.

Chapter Three

A Napkin?

WHAT EXACTLY IS a napkin? What is a napkin used for? Why do we need to use a napkin?

Part in knowledge and part in complete sarcasm, I am eager and ready to address the questions at hand. I am also in disbelief and shock over the fact that for many people, young and old alike, there is no completely correct way to answer these questions in a manner that will be both convincible and acceptable in the world of today. We all live in hope that everyone does know what a napkin is; but most likely, that knowledge is an assumption and we all know what the word assume means. So, rather than assume, allow me to simply state that by definition, a napkin is an object, preferably soft to the touch and easy to handle, to be used on one's face and hands, as a tool to assist in the removal of food or drink left behind, gathered by fingers and hands, dropped from a plate, or left in the corners of one's mouth, on to one's lap, or plastered on one's face while engaging in a meal.

There we have it! Wordy, but simple and quite clear, don't you agree?

Unfortunately everyone does not agree.

Oh, the joy of seeing the aftereffects of a fine meal or a snack on the sleeves or lap of the people around you. The racing stripes of grease from a crispy fried chicken leg or the brilliance of a rich and cheesy tomato sauce dripping off a slice of pizza and spreading like oil paint on the legs of a new pair of slacks or the front of a blouse or skirt. And then, just as we are feeling as if there is nothing else that could possibly be shared, the flash of a human arm, racing quickly across one's mouth, in hopes of collecting anything left behind and once again landing onto a lap below. And the napkin, untouched by human hands until that very moment is then dropped square and center in the middle of the plate, to be used as a camouflage or a blanket, to hide the pieces of food that have not been eaten or to sop up any liquid that remains on the plate.

If we thought long and hard, there is nothing that comes to mind that could be a greater insult, or as said in today's world, the ultimate slam, to the chef or the host/hostess of a meal, than to witness this kind of behavior at a dining table.

From the beginning, you are invited to the table, and everyone has taken a seat, properly of course—sitting tall in their seats, feet on the floor—and the meal is about to begin. The first thing you do is pick up and unfold the napkin by holding it at two corners then gently shaking it out to the side of your meal space and definitely away from the table. Finally, you complete the motion by placing the napkin over your lap.

Again, over your lap; not to be left folded and placed on your lap, sounding the horns and alerting the media that you have no intention of using the napkin during the meal. The proper position of the napkin at the place setting is at the left of the plate and this should be instruction enough of its use. A napkin, cloth or paper, is placed by your plate in your meal space. Hum, could this mean that the napkin is to be used as a cloth to wipe your mouths and your hands? I wonder. Alright, let's review the facts by saying that every household has its preference for the type of napkins that will be used at the dining table. Cloth or paper or anything in between, a napkin is a napkin, and a napkin does have a very important and specific purpose.

Fact: During the course of a meal, perhaps the portion of food that is picked up on a fork or spoon may just be a bit too large for one's mouth. This is sometimes referred to as the hungry-man approach to eating quickly and can only be determined and controlled by you individually. If the portion you have placed on your eating utensil is too large to fit in your mouth in one simple motion, which will most assuredly leave evidence behind, there is a perfect solution.

The napkin is there to rescue you. Of course, the hungry-man approach to eating is not suggested; but if the situation has presented itself, and everyone is looking at you in anticipation of your next move, just pick up your napkin and use it to clean up the mishap or "miss hit," shall we say.

This less-than-desirable form of eating can be corrected with the assistance of your napkin. If for some reason this situation does occur, you can wipe the corners of your mouth, your lips, and sometimes your cheeks and chin, erasing the signs left behind by engaging in the hungry-man eating approach. This evidence of shoveling has possibly left a small sign of non-entry into your mouth—perhaps all over your face—but can be attended to quickly, without incident, by the use of your napkin. Simply bring the napkin up to your mouth, dust off the evidence, and then return the napkin to its proper place over your lap. We all are completely aware of how large our mouth is and how much we can comfortably place into our mouth, without losing anything along the way. This napkin solution is only a suggestion, offered when the approach to your mouth is miscalculated and you are now sitting at the table and sharing the mishap with those seated around you.

Fact: It is not suggested to practice the hungry-man eating approach just because you are in a hurry and wish to complete the meal at Mach speed. Before you try to shove the larger-than-life bite into your mouth, back up and take another approach on the runway to your mouth, in a more suitable fashion.

Fact: It is not acceptable to use the napkin as a bath towel while at the dining table. When using your napkin to pat the areas around your mouth, use it gently. The neatly folded stack of fluffy cotton towels in the restroom around the corner of the dining space are to be used following a bath or a shower.

Fact: It is never acceptable to use your napkin as a tissue or hankie to wipe or blow your nose. If you have a stuffy head from a cold or allergies, excuse yourself from the table, walk into the restroom, close the door behind you, pick up a tissue, and blow to your heart's content. If you have to sneeze, it is more acceptable to block the sneeze with a napkin than with your hands; but please hold off on clearing your stuffy head until you are safely away from the dining table and have a tissue in hand.

Fact: It is not acceptable to use your napkin as a means of storage or a hiding place for any leftovers on your plate or food that you do not wish to eat. To wrap up food that you did not choose to finish during mealtime because you are too full or simply will not honor the no-thank-you helping rule, does not give you permission to use your napkin as a seaweed wrap on a sushi roll. Simply leave what you choose not to eat on your plate in open sight. There is no need for the food bits to be covered. It will be much easier for the host/hostess or your mom to do the cleanup at the end of the meal if she doesn't have to go on a scavenger hunt.

Fact: It is not acceptable to use a napkin as a hot pad to hold food items while you are at the table. If finger food is served and is too hot to hold comfortably, wait until it cools down; patience is the path to take.

When you are invited to the dining table, at home or away, upon your arrival, take your seat. There should always be a napkin placed in your meal space, for your use only, and the napkin is most often placed at the left of your plate. Take the napkin by two corners and shake the fold loose to the side of your meal space, than place the napkin over your lap.

At a formally set table, the fork(s) will be placed first with the folded napkin to the left. If a charger or show plate is used, the napkin may be placed on top of this plate.

At an informally set table, the fork(s) may be placed on top of the folded napkin.

When the sitting arrangement has limited meal space, the napkin may be placed on top of the meal plate or directly on the table in between the flatware, if there is no plate yet on the table.

Whatever the seating arrangement or the style of dining may be, a napkin should always be placed in your meal space. Cloth or paper, the napkin is placed to the left of the plate or in the center of your meal space if there is no plate. And yes, as with most rules, there may be a few variables; however, with this rule, there is only one.

At special events, such as weddings, parties, celebrations, and, in some families, during the holidays, linens may be used as an element of design in the color palette or for decorative design, including the napkin. If this is the case, the napkin may be placed in the center of the charger or show plate, or placed in between the flatware at each place setting. When napkins are used as a form of décor, they are often folded in various configurations: a flower, a crown, or an envelope to hold a menu card, or perhaps a single flower. A napkin can also be contained by using a napkin ring, a tie with a ribbon or leaf, or a band kissed with a decorative element of design. And there is, of course, the famous rabbit ear napkin display. A rolled cloth napkin stuck inside a glass or coffee cup and placed at the top of the meal space, usually flopping over from one side to the other, looking back at you like a bunny standing at the side of the road waiting for its break to run in front of a car.

Over the years, you will probably be introduced to numerous styles of napkin folds, presented in many different manners, and you will all form your own opinions, determined by your likes and dislikes in the art of napkin placement and display. As you have probably picked up from my most recent splash of sarcasm, the bunny ear display, or what I refer to as the wrecked lazy rabbit roll, is not the most finished or recommended look for the placement of a napkin at any table. When seen, I might suggest that you go back to the basics and just place a folded napkin, formally or informally, at the left of the plate. But, for now, my apology is extended if I have offended anyone by expressing my opinion on the wrecked lazy rabbit presentation. And with my apology, in all fairness, I must add, that if you are planning a bunny theme for your event that does revolve around rabbits, wrecked, lazy, or otherwise, the rolled napkin display would probably be all right.

Now that we have reviewed the meaning of a napkin, its intended use and placement, and have mentioned a few suggestions on decorative forms for a napkin on the table, it is time to move on to another etiquette rule, which will address the second question: What to do with the napkin when one gets up from the table during the meal or when one has completed the meal?

First, it is important to address leaving the table during a meal.

You are seated at the dining table and you are called away; what do you do? If the calling is truly important, the first thing you do is always excuse yourself from the table to your host/hostess and to those around you. Then, fold your napkin and place it on the left side of your plate, in your meal space. Stand up and push your chair close to the table edge and then walk away.

I am confident that a group of you are shaking your heads and saying that folding the napkin is too time-consuming. Alright, then gather the napkin neatly and place it to the left of your meal space, ensuring that you are not intruding on the meal space of the person seated next to you. Fold or gather—your choice.

What about placing the napkin on the seat of their chair or hanging the napkin on the back of the chair? Is this acceptable? Not exactly, nor is it recommended for several reasons.

Let's say that you are called away from the table but before your departure, you choose to drop your napkin on the seat of your chair. Upon your return to the table, you may just forget that the napkin is resting in a pile on the seat of your chair and the next thing you know, you plop down on top of it, forcing you to stand up once again, or having to pull the napkin out from under your body. How attractive is that?

Perhaps you are away from home, at a party or special celebration of some kind, and you decide to hang your napkin on the back of your chair. A server or another guest may walk by your chair, knocking the napkin onto the floor. Then someone like me, or a server in the dining room, may pick the napkin up and toss it in the bag of "dirties," and justly so. Once a napkin has fallen on the floor in a public dining space, the thought of using the napkin on your mouth or fingers would probably not be the best idea, and it is most often replaced.

Common sense and proper etiquette would suggest that when leaving the table, it would be most appropriate to take a moment to fold or gather the napkin and place it to the left of your meal space. That way, you have easy access to the napkin upon your return.

And when the party is over and the guests are preparing to depart for the evening, repeat the motion by folding or gathering the napkin, then placing the napkin to the left of your meal space. It also makes it convenient for the servers to gather at the end of the evening.

Chapter Four

All That Silverware

WE CAN ALL relate to this subject. Just the thought of all that silverware can be very intimidating to anyone, especially when the fear becomes a reality, and we are placed in a situation of using the silverware properly. As we are looking down on more than one fork and one knife at the same time, and we begin to wonder what the heck we are supposed to do with all those pieces of shiny silverware, panic does set in!

Over the years, there have been occasions when I, too, have been invited to an evening event that is based around a fabulous meal, and as I glance down at the lavishly designed meal space that has been reserved in my honor, zeroing in on all of the shiny forks, knives, and spoons looking back at me as they lay perfectly placed to the left, the right, and above the plate, it does happen! For one split moment, the blood rushes to my head, my heart drops into my stomach, my breathing comes to a sudden halt, and I feel a blanket of sheer panic taking over. My first response is to immediately reach for my wine glass and after taking a very large, but lady-like gulp, the recorder in my mind saves the day, kicking back into my memory bank on a lesson learned long ago; I see my sweet Greek grandmother standing before me, calmly saying, "Begin with the outer and work your way inner. As for the ones at the top of your plate, finish your meal then use after dinner."

This is a true story, a bit corny, but still true. Now, please keep in mind that my sweet grandmother's English was less than perfect. In fact, in the sixty plus years she lived as an American citizen of the United States, she never did master the Queen's English. And as a result, this bit of wisdom was not presented in the most eloquent or proper of ways or even offered in full sentences for that matter. But the words were spoken by a true lady and the matriarch of our family, received loud and clear, and understood perfectly by everyone who heard them. Most of all, it made total and complete sense! It was a lesson in table manners and the proper use of silverware that was taught to me as a child, then passed down to my children and is now being taught to my grandchildren. A lesson that I have reflected on time and again; a safety net so to speak, that over the years, has been a comfort for my entire family whenever we see shiny pieces of silverware taking over our meal space anywhere and anytime. The point is that no matter how the message is presented in this lesson on table manners, there is a proper order of use and a proper placement in your meal space for each and every eating utensil. And as long as the lesson is learned by those it is presented to, the words of the lesson can be whatever you wish, because the meaning always remains the same.

A family story comes to mind where this message from my grandmother on the basics of good table manners and the use of silverware would have been most appropriate.

It was a holiday dinner at our home a long time ago. All three of our children were still in high school, and each had invited a guest to join in our holiday celebration, to share in the foods and traditions from both the Greek side and the traditional side of the holiday coin. A few of our friends were also invited to fill our home and share in the holiday festivities. The holiday was Easter Sunday. On very rare occasions, and this Sunday was to be one of those rare occasions, both Greek Easter and traditional Easter, fell on the same date.

A baked glazed ham, potatoes *dauphinois*, and fresh grilled asparagus, completed with a pineapple-upside-down cake topped with fresh whipped cream were all prepared, in honor of the traditional celebration. Roast leg of lamb, rice pilaf, and stuffed grape leaves with homemade yogurt, finished with a large platter of Greek pastry, including the most recognizable, *baklava*, were all prepared in honor of the Greek family traditions.

The table was set with crisp celery-green colored linens. The matching napkins, tied with a cello-wrapped chocolate Easter egg hand-decorated with royal frosting flowers and personalized with the name of each guest, were created with love, and also served as a place card at each table setting. Make no mistake, the ever-so-popular wrecked lazy rabbit napkins sticking out of a glass or cup were not invited to our Easter table.

The silverware, or as more commonly referred to, flatware, were limited but proper and most important, sufficient for the meal. A salad fork and a dinner fork, placed in the proper position on the left side of the dinner plate, to be used as intended throughout the duration of the dinner, as the salad, main entrees, and side dishes would be placed on the table in proper serving platters and bowls all at the same time, to be enjoyed in a family-style manner rather than served course by course.

A dinner knife and teaspoon were placed on the right side of the dinner plate; dinner knife first, with the cutting edge facing the rim of the plate and the teaspoon resting nicely to the right of the dinner knife. The dessert fork and second teaspoon, to be used for cake, pastries, and coffee following the meal, were both placed at the top of the plate at each place setting, with full knowledge that if there were to be questions about the shiny stuff, these two pieces of flatware would be the topic of conversation.

Finally, the napkin tied neatly with a soft pink double-faced satin ribbon and decorated with the handmade chocolate personalized egg, was positioned in the center of each dinner plate so guests could identify their seat merely by reading their name on the egg—cozy but comfortable and truly inviting. The china selected for the day was a lovely family collectible with pink flowers accented with green leaves and trim, perfectly matched to the linens and ribbon trim surrounding the chocolate eggs.

Three glass stems, or footed glasses, were placed at the knife point on the right side of each meal space; one water stem, one white wine stem, and one red wine stem to be used in a universal manner, or in layman terms, the same glass to be used for many services, for either the red wine paired with the lamb or the homemade pink lemonade, to be served to our under-aged guests. If space had allowed, there would have been a fourth stem for the lemonade and the red wine stem would then be used as intended, eliminating the use of a universal stem.

The floral arrangement, filled with the colors of spring time, was placed in the center of the table; serving plates and serving bowls, covered and open, filled and trimmed with all of the holiday goodies, were arranged neatly from one end of the table to the other, with sets of porcelain bunny salt and pepper shakers dancing in between. No candles to light, as dinner would begin and conclude before six o'clock—a subject that will be discussed in another chapter.

The table was festive and beautifully finished, and it was time to begin the celebration. As my husband invited our friends and family to the dining room, everyone found their seats, excited to see the many selections of foods and especially the big chocolate egg that had been personally decorated for every family member and friend invited to join us on this special occasion.

We were ready to begin our celebration when something very odd happened. For one moment, it was as if someone had abruptly turned down the volume of the music coming through a CD player, the room was still and there was complete silence. As I glanced over at my husband, I saw a little smirk take over his face, and as my eyes continued around the table, that same smirk could be seen on the faces of all three of our teenaged children, as if our family was painfully aware that all of our guests were patiently waiting for someone to make the first move. Then, altogether, as if orchestrated, each member of our family picked up his or her own napkin that was resting in the center of his or her dinner plate, releasing the personalized chocolate egg and placed the egg carefully to rest at the top of his or her place setting. With a quick shake to the side of their meal space, everyone placed their napkin over their laps. Then suddenly, as if a magic wand passed over the room, the silence was broken by the motion of the guests seated around our dining table, all following suit of the ritual of the placement of the napkin and our Easter dinner celebration began.

After a short blessing, the platters and serving dishes began to make their way around the table as each guest, carefully, and using the proper serving utensils for each item, placed a portion of the many choices of foods on their dinner plate. Subconsciously, my eyes were focused on the side plates at each place setting, watching in anticipation to see if by some strange miracle, the salad plate would be filled with salad and the bread plate would be the resting grounds for a crunchy bread roll and a whipped butter rosette.

Not a chance; apparently, the two side plates were considered "décor" and were left empty with one exception. Our daughter's friend carefully placed his personalized chocolate egg first on the bread and butter plate and then on the cushion of his chair—interesting decision. Then, out of nowhere, it happened again; when everyone had been served and all of the dinner plates were filled to their capacity, a complete cloud of silence hovered over our Easter dining table. I quickly turned my focus from the empty side plates to the faces of our guests and realized that everyone was again waiting for direction, a cue as to when and how to take that first bite.

Once again, my husband jumped in to save the day and immediately made his move by picking up his wine glass, offering a toast in honor of our guests and the holiday. As soon as the toast was over and everyone's glasses were placed back on the table, the gates opened and everyone slipped into their comfort zone and the "race was underway." Some of the guests gave a quick inspection of the eating utensils, decisions were made, and the meal began. A few of the guests went directly for their dinner fork, and with their knife held tightly in the opposite hand, began stabbing away at the meat of their choice, vigorously sawing back and forth in hopes of achieving that perfect cut. With meat sliding back and forth and eventually flying off their plates, the race continued, and it seemed as if our guests had all mounted their favored horse and were all racing for the finish line. One lovely young lady chose to use her salad fork for the entire meal—the mini utensil, I suppose. Possibly because it was the first utensil she picked up or perhaps it was because it was the smallest of the forks, and she was a tiny-framed person, who knows! And one of the adult guests decided to use the dessert teaspoon that was resting at the top of the dinner plate, assisted by the butter knife, in a push and scoop motion—the bulldozer manner of eating known to some, never releasing either utensil until his or her plate was empty.

The rumbling sounds of everyone talking back and forth, yet nothing could be understood, and the clattering of the flatware hitting the china filled the entire room. And as the race continued, and my eyes circled the dining table, I must admit it was truly a front-row seat for the best sport in the world, the sport of people watching. Meat sailing from plate to table, the seesaw sounds of the aggressive attempts to cut the perfect bite, and the display of use of the knives and forks were most entertaining. Spoons, forks, and even knives, held like shovels or scoops rather than eating utensils, and the unexpected opportunity for all to experience meal consumption in the fast and furious modern way, filled the dining room.

And elbows, for some strange reason, it was all about the elbows—on the table, invading the meal space of the person sitting beside you, on the edge of the table holding that ever-so-heavy fork, knife, and head. There were arms flying in every direction; reaching across the table for the tiny bunny salt and pepper shakers, a crunchy roll, or a second helping from the many platters and bowls placed down the center of the table. And double-dipping, lots of double-dipping. We were even fortunate enough to experience the crash, and then flood, of pink lemonade knocked across the table, spilling directly into the basket of the crunchy bread rolls. Truly a dining experience to remember.

And then, as quickly as the race had begun, the approach to the finish line was in full motion. The conclusion of this very unique manner of dining and the enjoyment of the steady stream of unidentifiable conversation came to an end. And one by one, each guest stood up from the table; a few of the guests mumbling a quiet "thanks for the great food," and with the drop of the napkins, directly into the center of the empty dinner plates below or on the seat of the chairs once occupied, now pushed up against the dining room table, and our guests disappeared into the family room to catch up on the score of a basketball game that was in full play on the wide-screen TV. If I remember correctly, one of our adult guests grabbed a crunchy bread roll soaked in pink lemonade just before his exit from the table. I guess he needed something to munch on during the game.

Oh my gosh! Talk about the ideal opportunity to ask the age old question, "Where IS your mother?" This was a true and entertaining Easter celebration at the Brown residence. At this time, I do feel obligated to insert a very important comment. This dinner was not a planned opportunity for research on my book, nor was it a gathering of control or criticism; on the contrary, our

Easter dinner was intended to be a warm and welcome invitation to a holiday dinner, in fact a double holiday dinner with the anticipated excitement of meeting a few special friends of our children and sharing the company of our friends. A dinner to celebrate with good conversation, great food, and family tradition in our home.

And the moral of this story? Although it sounds like an afternoon of total chaos taking place right before our very eyes, or a home version of the last stretch at the Kentucky Derby, that was really not the case, nor the intended case. In fact, this hands-on introduction to the fast and furious modern consumption of a meal was a learning experience, played out innocently and calmly, with confidence by each and every guest, as if this type of table behavior was "the norm" and was practiced every day, everywhere a meal was taken.

Fact: We all know that not everyone in this day and age knows, or is expected to understand the "what-fork-and-which-knife-do-we-use" thing. And no one is expected to be able to apply the lesson correctly each and every time a meal is served without that knowledge.

But this particular holiday experience was a perfect example of how important the application of the basic steps of good manners are. A strong reminder that the lessons in the proper use of eating utensils, beginning in your home at a very young age, will someday all come together, making perfect sense and, as a result, will be an enjoyable and pleasant surprise for you and for those around you. It doesn't matter if this lesson on eating utensils is presented with elegance or in broken sentences. Begin with the outer and work your way inner. As for the ones at the top of your plate, finish your meal, then use after dinner. As long as the lesson is direct and to the point, that is all that is required. Consistency and practice will make the difference.

Think about it. If there are five courses to your meal, you begin with the flatware that has been placed at the far left and the far right of your plate. As the courses are served, you work your way, piece by piece, toward the dinner plate.

Begin from the outer and work your way inner, until you reach the center of your meal space, which once again is your dinner plate.

At the center of your meal space will be the last of your dinner eating utensils that were once placed left and right of your meal space, and should also be the last course of your meal, before dessert, of course.

Dessert, which is often served with coffee, and follows the last course of your meal, is when the second part of the lesson comes into play.

As for the ones at the top of your plate, finish your meal, then use after dinner.

Simple? I knew it would be, and now you are ready to enjoy a meal anywhere, even at the Ritz. Always remember, a meal is the time to gather around a dining table, sharing time with the people you care about. A time for great conversation and a time to enjoy the foods that have been prepared for you. Gathering around a dining table is even more enjoyable for everyone if you use the eating utensils properly!

Here is a good suggestion that can be used as a tool to teach children about eating utensils and their proper use. Have the children set the table while you are preparing the meal. Give them all the proper utensils that will be used for the meal you are planning and guide them in the proper placement of the pieces. Most of us all have dishwashers so there are no worries about the cleanup. If you, as a parent, teach these basic and simple lessons of good table manners and the proper use of flatware to your children and are consistent, you will soon see that practice does make perfect and you can be assured that each and every time a meal is served thereafter, the experience will be more enjoyable for everyone. I promise.

We have now made a dent on the subject of eating utensils, and have reviewed the order of placement of the flatware in our meal space and the order each piece of flatware is to be used, simply and clearly.

The next step is to visit the many types of flatware and their proper use. But first, take a step back in time for a little history lesson, establishing what an eating utensil is, a short review of the many names for such utensils.

Eating utensils are things that many of us take for granted. Every household has a drawer filled with them, but, surprisingly, modern eating utensils took years to develop.

According to the California Academy of Science (CAS) Department of Anthropology, people have used knives for eating as well as for hunting, food preparation, and defense since prehistoric times. People used knives to spear their food and then bring it to their mouths. In the middle ages, most people carried a knife in a sheath attached to a belt. A knife as we think of it today would have been different in size, shape, and consistency, but most importantly in purpose. A spear or arrow-shaped blade, again made by hand out of wood, stone, or bone, was used for the hunt and kill of the meal as its main purpose, followed only in second place by chopping or cutting, if one was prepared to do so and the need was present. We all have seen pictures of a knife being used as an eating utensil—stabbing and holding firmly the catch of the day, as it was consumed. And, unfortunately, there are still some people today who use a knife in exactly that same manner. No, that is not the proper way to use a knife, so let's just get that thought out of your mind. In any event, the utensils from the prehistoric age were created for the specific purposes needed at that time and used accordingly. No fancy engravings or frills in shape or design—a useful tool created for a specific need. The CAS reports that Greeks were the first to develop forks to help carve and serve meat. These forks were large and had two tines, much like serving forks of today. In the seventh century, royal courts in the Middle East began using forks at the dinner table and from the twelfth century, wealthy Byzantines brought them to Italy. Spoons have been used since Paleolithic times according to the CAS, often made of shells or wood. The Greek and Latin word for spoon was derived from *cochiea*, which means shell.

As our civilization evolved and progressed and our personal habits became more sophisticated and refined, eating utensils moved forward as well, and these utensils were called "silverware," mainly because the material used to create these eating and serving utensils was made out of sterling silver or silver over pewter. The look of the utensil became important, inviting detailed designs and decorative accents to be added to the many pieces, resulting in a variety of patterns and styles to choose from. And as the climb up the ladder of social status and position progressed, more and more defined pieces of silverware were produced for every food item and purpose imaginable. As time passed, the cost of silver became out of reach for the average working family and an alternative metal was discovered. Stainless steel was used in the production of eating and service utensils. Again, detailed designs and decorative accents were included and pieces were made in various weights, which would determine the cost per place setting or item. Stainless steel still remains a desirable substitute for everyday use. Much to the dismay of silversmiths, many of the silver patterns have been duplicated in the alternative metals, such as Wallace, Grand Baroque, or Towle Old Colonial and, surprisingly, they are lovely and durable in both metals.

Then came plastic, a disposable, cost-efficient product, used in the production of eating utensils and some serving pieces, hopefully used for very casual, outside "throw-another-shrimp-on-the-barbie"-style functions. Yes, plastic flatware can be time and cost efficient for the host/hostess, however, please do not mistake these disposable plastic items as comparable substitutes for silver or stainless steel. Disposable plastic flatware is limited in patterns and design and is far from sturdy, so a word of warning, please do not plan on cutting your meat successfully with a plastic knife; it usually does not happen with success. And certainly, do not count on reusing disposable plastic unless you like that moisture-stain and scratched look.

Eating utensils are referred to by many names; silverware and flatware are probably the most common. The word *silverware* is actually referring to a high quality and more costly metal used in the production of eating utensils and serving pieces. Stainless steel, the more practical, alternative metal used in the production of eating utensils and serving pieces, would probably not be the proper word to use, as first, it makes no sense, and second, it may become a point of contention for the host/hostess who has invested his or her life savings in the purchase of fine sterling silver flatware and would really not appreciate hearing the words *lovely stainless steel* as a compliment to her investment. Hence, the proper and most acceptable term when referring to eating utensils that should make everyone happy is flatware. It is flat and it serves as tableware; the word *ware* is the saving grace. Similar to saying silverware—silver is the metal and ware is its use. So with that bit of information, we will now refer to all eating utensils as flatware as we continue on with this topic.

Many years ago, I inherited a set of sterling silver flatware, dating back to the eighteenth century. As many of the pieces of flatware are no longer used in today's world, and were unfamiliar to me, the search began to identify all of the eating and serving utensils and their intended uses. There were dozens, literally dozens of individual pieces of flatware that created a complete and full place setting, which apparently in the eighteenth century, filled the meal space for each guest at a formal dining table. As I looked down at all of those shiny pieces of silverware, placed properly to the left, right, and at the top of the charger plate, once again, sheer panic took over! Can you imagine the number of food courses and the size of the meal space needed to accommodate eight forks, eight knives, and spoons of all sizes and shapes, at each place setting? Forks for trout, for salads, large and small, and for sardines; a fish fork, a lemon fork, an olive fork, and a berry fork; all different shapes and styles and all with an exact purpose and intent. There were ramekin forks, a lobster fork, an oyster fork, and an individual beef fork, and the list went on. At the bottom of the box, I found scoops for marrow, knives for cold and hot meat, for duck and for pheasant, and spoons in every shape and size, all to be used in a very unique way. As I continued to dig through the box of silverware, it soon became my quest to conquer the use and purpose of all of the many pieces, and the journey to find a book or some form of printed information that could answer all of my questions launched at full speed.

After many years of searching, I came across a book detailing one-hundred and twenty-three pages of individual silverware pieces and an additional thirty-two pages explaining the use of the myriad serving pieces created in my silver pattern alone. I was totally fascinated and threatened all at the same time. As I continued to rummage through the silver pieces, trying to make sense of it all, it came to me. Knowledge is great, but why all the pressure?

And I realized that learning everything there is to know about the wonderful piece of history surrounding my treasure, were lessons that would be cherished and held close to my heart; but the fact remains that my table is not large enough to accommodate all of the pieces of silverware for one place setting, let alone a table set for company. However, if by some chance, I would be invited to attend a dinner at the White House or perhaps to dine with the Queen, I would be confident in knowing precisely what to do with each and every piece of all that silverware. And so, with a big sigh of relief and the personal satisfaction that my quest for knowledge had been conquered, I realized that the information I had discovered could now be carefully filed in my memory bank for future use, and I could carefully place the silverware in a very safe place and go on my merry way.

Although there are hundreds of different pieces of flatware, and each with a specific purpose, it is probably appropriate to address with description a few of the more commonly used pieces of flatware, so when encountering a meal space filled with that shiny stuff, one can attack the situation with simplicity and confidence.

Let's begin with the fork. The four most commonly used forks in today's society are:

- A dinner fork
- A salad fork
- A dessert fork
- A cocktail fork

Any of these four forks will have a minimum of two prongs and usually no more than five prongs, extending out from the body or bowl of the utensil. Each fork will also have a handle; some are more comfortable to hold and manipulate than others. Design, engraving, and monogramming may or may not appear on a fork as décor; but has no bearing on the function or use of this utensil. Forks will be placed to the left of the plate, in the order of their use. And when you see more than one fork in your meal space, remember the lesson on their use and the meal will be an enjoyable and comfortable experience: *Begin with the outer and work your way inner.*

A dinner fork paired with a dinner knife are used together when cutting bite-size portions of food and bringing the food to your mouth. In the Western world, if you are right-handed and you wish to cut a bite-size piece of meat from your serving, the fork is usually held in the left hand, prong side down, holding the food item while it is being cut, allowing full control of the item on the plate. The knife, properly held, would be in the right hand. When the piece of meat is successfully cut, the knife is placed at the top of the dinner plate, blade edge toward the center of the plate, and the fork is switched to the right hand for the approach to your mouth. If you are left-handed, switch hands and follow the same procedure. Abroad or in other parts of the world, if you are right-handed, the fork is held and remains in the left hand, prong side down; using the knife, which is held by the right hand, to push the food item on the back of the fork; the fork then makes its approach to your mouth.

And when a bite-size portion of food requires cutting once again, the fork remains in the left hand, prong side down and the knife remains in the right hand—no switching of the fork. This technique is commonly referred to as the European technique. Remember, one rule remains the same and that rule is that the pieces of flatware are held at an angle when cutting or eating bite-size portions of food. The "Stab down" approach is not the path to take.

It is unacceptable to hold the handle of any eating utensil like a shovel. The length of the handle, when in your service hand, should rest in the bend of your thumb and forefinger, prong side up. At the end of the meal, place the fork on the inside position of the knife, which has already been placed at the top of the dinner place. The prong side of the fork is facing upward. Never place a used eating utensil on the table beside your dinner plate; there is no exception to this etiquette rule.

The knife has an obvious primary purpose and that is for cutting, and once again, if using the European technique, to push the food onto the back of the fork, never leaving the hand. If the Western technique is a more suitable and comfortable manner for you, follow the procedure for that method. Unlike our ancestors of prehistoric times, a knife is never used in the same manner as a fork; it is used to cut or push the food items from your plate and nothing more. When using your knife for cutting, hold the knife properly and go easy on the back-and-forth sawing motions. Use nice, gentle cuts; muscle power is not needed to cut a simple piece of food.

Because there are so many types of spoons, following the rules in the lesson on proper use can assist you in using the proper spoon with the proper course. Once again, the spoon is held and used in the hand you are gifted in. If you are right-handed, hold the spoon in your right hand. If you are left-handed, hold the spoon in your left hand; in both forms, the length of the handle resting in the web between your thumb and forefinger, bowl side up. There is no shoveling or scooping. And once again, when you have completed the meal, place the spoon on the inside of the fork that is resting at the top of your plate, next to the knife, bowl side up, and never place a used spoon on the table.

When in doubt as to the proper use of flatware, jiggle the key to your memory back and pull out the lesson taught by my grandmother and shared in this chapter. If you are still confused, just look around at the guests seated at the table, and you can be assured that someone is following the steps of the flatware lesson, and the rest is up to you. The proper use of flatware is a lesson that should be taught as a child and encouraged at each and every meal. Mealtime should be enjoyable and that enjoyment should be shared with those around you. The shovel, or hungry-man approach are both unacceptable displays of bad manners, and the stabbing and sawing methods when using a knife are equally undesirable. After this lesson, bad manners at the table will be a thing of the past. Hold your flatware properly, serve yourself politely, get the hungry-man and shovel approach out of your head, and what will follow will be a perfect display of good manners, leaving you confident in knowing that what you are doing is proper and correct.

Chapter Five

Table Taboos

POSTED ON THE wall of the lunch room at the elementary school my granddaughter attends, is a handmade sign that reads:

No chewing with your mouth open

No talking with food in your mouth

No taking food from your neighbor's plate

No running around in the lunchroom

All very good and simple rules that can be added to the *Table Taboos* list, and obviously rules that are being enforced and followed by the elementary students, kindergarten through fifth grade, at this school. However, as you look around the dining table at a restaurant or even in your own home, these rules are pretty much hit and miss more frequently than not.

As far back as we can remember we have always been taught to share. Share your toys with your brother. Share your books with your sister. Share your ball on the playground. Share your candy with your friends

But at the dining table, the rule of sharing is more structured. While it is a nice gesture to share books and toys with others as a child, and equally as nice to let the neighbor borrow the lawnmower or the family down the street use the swimming pool floaters, when occupying a meal space at the dining table, there are rules that social etiquette and basic simple grace will encourage, stating that you do not share.

The *Table Taboo* list is very basic and the items on the list are guided by good common sense. But we have all been witness to some major dining table taboos; so once again, a review of the basics of good manners, or more appropriately put, the no-brainier rules that say it is not proper to share at any dining table, are soon to unfold.

First on the "no sharing at the table" list is one that is usually accompanied by delightful sound effects, that when heard, will immediately flag the situation at hand with a big "what are you thinking?"—an act that is commonly displayed as frequently by adults as it is by children, at home and away from home. Let's get started.

BLOWING YOUR NOSE AT THE TABLE

Blowing your nose at the table is probably one of the most obvious displays of absolutely no manners known to anyone and should not only be at the top of the *Table Taboo* list, but should also be listed number one on the no-brainier list. It is a crude personal act that should never be performed while at the dining table or even in public for that matter. This subject was briefly talked about in chapter three; however, the subject certainly demands far more attention than just a short paragraph.

Alright, you have congestion in your head and whether this congestion is from a head cold or allergies, the old head feels like a water balloon that is about to burst. And you just happen to be sitting at the table when the sudden urge takes over your better sense telling you to relieve the pressure, and the best way to accomplish that relief is by blowing your nose. We all understand that a stuffy head is probably not the most comfortable feeling, but for heaven's sake, don't relieve that pressure at the dining table! Excuse yourself from the table and walk into the next room, preferably the restroom. Close the door behind you and blow to your heart's content. When you feel the urge, take a moment and observe the space around you, and you will quickly be reminded that the time and the place for this type of crude relief is all wrong!

The time is wrong because when at the dining table, you partake in conversation and enjoy the meal placed before you. You do not share disgusting sounds with your table neighbors.

And, the place is definitely all wrong because as one can clearly see, the table does not have a luxurious counter top with a color coordinated box of tissue placed on it, and we all know that a tissue is the most important item required to tackle the job of clearing your head.

If the observation is continued, you will discover that there is no trash can to be found, on or near the dining table, and that form of receptacle, used to dispose the tissue after the job, is a must!

And as the little switch on your memory bank kicks into high gear, you will experience sheer panic at the very thought of tackling this naughty deed at the table. The information filed neatly in your memory bank will remind you once again, that the napkin resting over your lap must remain over your lap and should never be used for relieving your stuffy head, so no need to even go in that direction. Just remember that tissue! Excuse yourself from the table, and stand up and walk into the next room and take care of business.

Quite frankly, as a host/hostess, vintage napkin or not, if anyone chose to use the napkin for their nose, that napkin would end up in the trash without question, and as for the guest—I would certainly wait until the guest had the opportunity to read this book before he or she was invited back into our home for a meal.

Sharing is a wonderful courtesy that we are taught as children; sharing the experience and the sounds of clearing your stuffy head and nose, on the other hand, are far from wonderful or polite, and should never be encouraged or accepted by anyone while sitting at the dining table. Yuck! Just the visual of this action is too much for most of us to handle, especially while trying to enjoy a good meal.

Chewing With Your Mouth Open or Talking With Your Mouth Full

Now here are two additional acts that must be added to the *Table Taboos* list. When people are seated around the dining table, one must remember that everyone present is perfectly capable of enjoying all of the delicious food items that they desire on their own plate and in their own meal space.

They also have their own napkin to be used when necessary, for their own mishaps if any, and there is no need to borrow the napkin next door. So when you think about it, there really is no need for anyone to share by spewing bits of food from his or her mouth, which is exactly what happens if one insists on talking with his or her mouth full or chewing with his or her mouth open.

The first rule of good table manners is: chew with your mouth closed, followed closely by no talking with your mouth full.

When these rules are ignored, bits of food fly uncontrollably everywhere! Tiny particles of spinach or pieces of spaghetti, shooting across the table from a cannon that happens to be an open mouth, is unacceptable and talking with a full mouth of food is just plain rude.

Just a little FYI. The term seafood, spelled "s-e-a," like the ocean, is appropriate at the dining table only when it refers to a fish selection, prepared then placed in the center of a dinner plate. "See food" is the disgusting by-product of speaking with your mouth full of food, so that with every word that comes out, your dinner companions get to catch glimpses of the mushy mess that you are trying to chew as you hold a conversation. It is rude and unappealing and should always be considered a big fat *No-No*.

Solution to the firing-range-effect: When sitting at the dining table, always chew with your mouth closed and never talk with your mouth full. You already have a captive audience with the people sitting at the dining table with you. No one is going anywhere until the meal is completed so sit tight, take your time and alternate:

One bite of food and swallow
A few words of conversation
One bite of food and swallow
A few words of conversation

THAT'S MY MEAL!

Have you ever been invited to a lovely restaurant and after much deliberation over the extravagant menu, you finally make a decision on exactly what will tickle your fancy? You carefully place your menu order and the server soon places a plate in the meal space in front of you—you are delighted. Then out of nowhere, a fork comes flying across the dining table and lands right in the middle of your pasta, swirling a mound of the anticipated enjoyment placed before you, stealing just a little taste. What you have now experienced is yet another item from the *Table Taboos* list. Good grief! If the meal you selected was one that you wanted to share with the person seated across the table from you or anyone else for that matter, you would have requested additional plates, sharing plates. And if that is not bad enough, this *Table Taboo* has two sides to the story.

First, your meal space is just that, your meal space, and what you have on your plate is for you.

Second, if it has been established that it is not proper to reach across the table and help yourself to another person's meal, then reaching across the table and taking food from a serving platter, using your personal fork, rather than the serving utensil that should be on the platter, because you feel that you only want "a little taste," is surely one more for the *Table Taboo* list. Your personal fork is just that, your personal fork—to be used on your personal plate in your personal meal space. No sharing bites, stabs, or anything else that may be hidden in your mouth or behind your teeth!

And a serving platter is a serving platter, and should have its own serving utensils. Keep your personal fork personal, and use the serving utensil that has been placed on the serving platter for that purpose.

DOUBLE-DIPPING

I am confident that you have all heard the term, double-dipping. If this term was being used at an ice cream parlor, double-dipping would mean two deep dips into a tub of chocolate sauce, creating a double thick coating of chocolate decadence over a mountain of soft swirl ice cream. However, at the dining table, double-dipping is another *Table Taboo*. The double approach to dipping with a potato chip into a container of onion dip or a veggie stick into a bowl of dill-flavored sour cream, seems to be a four-step process, probably created by a person who was too lazy to pick up a plate and place a personal serving of dip on his plate; four improper steps that when practiced, can guarantee that the bowl of dip you are double-dipping in, will not be touched by anyone else but you.

First into the dip
Second into the mouth
Third, into the dip
And then in the mouth again

Now, close your eyes and really get the full effect of what has just occurred, then think. Do you really want to dip your chip or veggie into onion dip or sour cream after someone else has been double-dipping? I highly doubt it. A great opportunity to experience double-dipping would be when *crudités*, or baskets of chips, are displayed on a table for self-service. The chips are large and crispy and the tray of fresh veggies are all larger than bite-size and one dive into the dip will not cover the entire item. So what do you do? Properly.

A. Double-dip as noted above

or

B. Pick up one of the little plates that were placed on the table of *hors d'oeuvres*, then using the serving spoon that has been placed in the dips, serve yourself a nice serving on your plate and take from that serving. Your own mobile meal space so to speak; and you can double-dip to your hearts content.

or

C. If there are no little *hors d'oeuvre* plates, make the ultimate sacrifice and just dip once or go *"al natural"* and skip the dip!

There are two correct answers to this question: B or C. While the double-dipping method may be enjoyed solo, you can be assured that anyone else who may wish to enjoy the dip following the solo venture double-dipping dive into the dip, will think twice about it.

This is Not Musical Chairs

Common sense should remind you that if it is not proper to share bits of food from an open mouth or take food from a neighbor's plate or from a serving platter with your personal fork, and that the sole purpose of a napkin is to be used for your personal mishaps at the table, and that your flatware is precisely your flatware, then it should make perfect sense that your chair is for your use only as well.

The seat of a dining chair is usually sixteen to twenty-four inches wide, and for a child, that may be a bit roomy. But as a child grows into his or her adult self, the chair size will be perfect. Therefore, even as a child, the dining chair that you occupy while seated at the dining table, is your chair! And at the table, everyone will remain seated for the duration of the meal.

The dining table is not the setting for the game musical chairs, so there is no need to jump up and down or to walk around. Sit down and enjoy the food that has been prepared in your honor. Also, no squirming, and especially no sharing of the chair space. Everyone at the table should have their own chair, and this good manner rule suggests you use it.

Good table manners are the basis of the lesson, and good old common sense is the guiding factor. When at the dining table, avoid the *Table Taboos* and enjoy the wonderful meal and the great company around you, keeping your meal space yours. And remember that everything, including the dining chair, within your meal space, belongs to you.

In the last few chapters, we have touched on several subjects pertaining to etiquette at the table. We have reviewed the importance of sitting at the table properly; what to do with your napkin and what to do with all that silverware. We have also covered proper behavior while at someone else's table and the *Table Taboo* list. So, here is a question for you:

You are having dinner with some friends in a lovely restaurant and in the middle of dinner, nature calls. What would do you?
  A. You silently stand up, drop your napkin on the seat of your chair, and quickly walk away from the table in hopes that no one will notice your departure.
  B. You politely excuse yourself, jump out of your chair, dropping your napkin in the center of your dinner plate because you have already completed that course, then walk away from the table.
  C. You politely excuse yourself, fold your napkin and place it to the left of your plate, stand up and push your chair in towards the edge of the table in your meal space, and depart.

Correct answer is C: When leaving the dinner table prior to the completion of a meal for any reason, you politely excuse yourself, fold your napkin and place it to the left of your plate, stand up and push your chair in towards the edge of the table in your meal space, and depart. That way, when you return to the table, there is no mystery as to your brief disappearance, no one has tripped over your chair left in the center of the room, and when you are again seated, your napkin can be again be placed over your lap with minimum effort and the meal will continue. Perfect—lesson learned.

Chapter Six

When to Give a Gift

LET'S BE HONEST, we all love to receive gifts, no matter how old we are. For most ladies, the excitement of seeing *Tiffany's* little aqua-blue box, tied perfectly with a double-faced, white satin ribbon, can take our breath away. For a child, the anticipation of opening brightly wrapped gifts surrounding the base of the tree on Christmas morning, is first and foremost in his or her mind. As that special birthday approaches or as Hanukkah or Christmas is peeking around the corner, the excitement of the gifts, followed by the celebration of the event, is the energy that engulfs us all and is the topic of conversation for weeks before and after the special day. Although it may seem somewhat materialistic, the warmth of these emotions wraps around us like a fluffy blanket. Gifts are like magic energy, and it is perfectly acceptable to enjoy a shot of its energy from time to time.

Most of us have been taught that on birthdays, Hanukkah, Christmas, weddings, or showers, a gift is given to a special someone in honor of that day. These are a few of the more obvious occasions where giving a gift is appropriate—and in most cases socially expected. But let's talk about the other occasions, the occasions when we ask ourselves: Is it appropriate to give a gift or not? What kind of a gift should be given? How much should be spent on a gift?

If a gift were to be given for each and every event, gathering, or celebration, we would be spending our entire lives at the mall or in specialty stores looking for the perfect gift, not to mention the fact that a very large bank account would be necessary to support these daily shopping sprees. If this were the case, in spite of how much most of us enjoy shopping, the gift-giving thing would never end, and we would be forced to sell all of our worldly goods or rob a bank to support the habit. Fortunately, this is not the case, so remove the signs for the garage sales and get rid of the blueprints for the bank on the corner—there is a proper answer.

Like all questions relating to proper etiquette and social grace in society, there is a time and a place for everything, including gift giving; hopefully, the following pages will make the gift-giving thing a bit easier to understand.

When looking up the word *gift* in the dictionary, the definition simply states: "a thing given" and also "the act or the instance of giving." The meaning seems easy enough to understand, yet most people are still in the clouds about when it is appropriate to give a gift, what type of gift should be given for the occasion, and how much they should spend. The answers to the last two questions are left up to the givers—you and me. However, for the question of when it is proper to give a gift, or whether a gift is even necessary, there are basic guidelines that are directed by etiquette, social and proper, suggesting when and why a gift is given.

Making the decision as to when a gift is given—and what type of gift it should be—can be overwhelming, and usually the end result is not giving a gift at all. This decision should not be an ordeal that results in nothing. By following a few simple and basic guidelines, the questions once consuming our brains, will transform into an enjoyable adventure that will be accepted and appreciated by the person you have honored with the gift and will receive the stamp of approval from etiquette experts around the world.

Remember the time you accepted an invitation to a party for a friend, and you walked in the door holding nothing but your winter coat in your hands? Oh my, not a memory that puts a smile on your face, correct?

We can all agree that there is nothing more awkward than attending a function where a gift of some kind is expected and most definitely appropriate, and there you are, standing in a corner, holding nothing that remotely resembles a gift of any kind, in hopes that no one will notice that first, you even entered the room, let alone showed up empty-handed.

Using the word *gift* and applying its meaning simply, a gift can be something tangible or an action or a personal gesture that one gives to another as a token of appreciation for an action received, for an accomplishment made, or in honor of a special day. A gift also can be a thing offered or received, in honor of a celebration or in memory of a special person. Are we all still together?

We all are aware of obvious gift-giving occasions, probably because we have all been on the receiving end of such an action, but other occasions are not so apparent. So I thought it would be helpful to make this gift-giving thing as simple as eating cake, by making a list of suggestions. So, here it is—a starter list of a few other occasions when it is an appropriate time for that gift-giving thing.

- A thank you for an action or favor received
- In appreciation for something offered in honor of you or a family member
- In celebration of a special day or event
- In remembrance of a person you love or is loved by a person close to you

No matter what the occasion, whenever a gift is given, the gift should be given from the heart—with no expectations, no obligations, and no conditions, just simply and with joy. There are no rules or guidelines with regard to a gift's style, creativity, or purpose; the choice of the gift is up to you. And as for cost of the gift? That decision is also up to you. The most important rule to remember about gift giving is any gift that is given should be from the heart and hopefully, received by the heart.

When this simple rule of gift giving is your guide, the perfect gift, for the perfect occasion, presented to that perfect person, will be a wonderful, fulfilling, and fun experience. Now, let's get down to business.

Chapter Seven

A Thank You Gift

SOMETIMES, SAYING THANK you with only a card or note may not seem sufficient; this can only be determined by you. If you feel that you would like to take the next thank you step, perhaps a tangible gift would be appropriate. Depending on the occasion and situation, the type of thank you gift can vary, but any gift that is given must be from the heart. Make your gifts personal, a reflection of you, by putting a little of yourself in every gift you give; you will never go wrong if you follow this advice.

Let's say you just returned from vacation, and you entrusted the safety of your home to a friend, neighbor, or family member. Upon your return, you found that this someone did an outstanding job of making sure that everything was perfect in your absence. The daily mail and newspapers were brought into the house and stacked neatly in a box on the kitchen floor, and the flowers and lawn had been watered and cared for, welcoming you home. In return for the hard work and personal attention given to you by taking care of your home, you decide to do something special to say thank you. The first question that pops into your head is, "How can I say thank you to this person with something that they will really like?"

Once again, I have a few suggestions to get you started—simple, personal, and straight from the heart.

BAKED GOODIES

Baked goodies are always an excellent choice for a special thank you. How about cookies—big ones—or brownies filled with gooey caramels or fluffy marshmallow crème? Perhaps a cake or cupcakes filled with fresh berries or frosted with decadent fudge frosting would be perfect. Or a pie, with mounds of meringue or whipped cream, placed in a basket, on a fun plate, or in a cellophane wrap tied with a bow. Everyone enjoys goodies, and homemade goodies are a delicious gift that says thank you directly from the heart of your family, the family kitchen—a special, sweet treat letting someone know that you wanted to do something very special by creating a yummy gift especially in his or her honor. If you don't bake, it's not a problem; there are markets, bakeries, and even warehouse stores that offer the most delightful baked goods. Just make a shopping run, and your problem is solved!

Fresh Fruit or Vegetables

Fresh fruit or garden vegetables are a colorful and inventive gift for anyone. A basket or container of fresh fruit or veggies wrapped in cello wrap and finished with a lovely ribbon or raffia bow can bring a fresh surprise to any household. Include a favorite family recipe using those fruits or vegetables. This special touch can bring families together, and is a personal reminder that the gift was selected especially for someone special. The family recipe enclosed will make the gift everlasting.

Dried Fruits and Nuts

Are there no garden or lovely fruits or vegetables in season? Not to worry. Dried fruits and nuts can be equally as grand, and they last a long time. Just put a little thought into the gift and find a way to make it personal. Make the gift especially from your home to their home, and don't forget to enclose the thank you note.

We all can agree from personal experience, an edible thank you gift, whether it be fresh from the garden or creatively packaged and purchased from a store, can be delightful to receive. And with a cleaver presentation and a few personal finishing touches from the heart, the gift will be greatly enjoyed, right down to that last delicious piece in the basket.

Flowers and Floral Arrangements

Flowers can be fun. Can you think of anyone who doesn't like flowers? A bouquet of fresh flowers from your garden or from the corner stand, placed in a vase or fun container and finished with the ribbon of your choice, can adorn a credenza in an entry or dress the center of a feasting table in any home.

Flowers are a thank you gift that is filled with the colors of a rainbow and happiness of the morning sun—and if picked from a personal garden, a gift from the center of your heart. A gift of flowers can fill a space with love and even romance, can brighten any day, and can bring a smile to any face.

Perhaps a blooming pot of flowers or a plant lush in varied shades of green and foliage, placed in a hand-painted ceramic pot, a vintage tin, or a simple terra-cotta container, will fit perfectly with the decorative elements of a friend's personal patio. It is said that a gift that will bloom and continue to grow is a gift that lives on forever, and each time the gift creates another blossom or extends its leaves toward the morning sun, it will be a reminder of the appreciation and thoughtfulness behind the gift. Nice, don't you agree?

A GIFT OF FRAGRANCE

A gift of fragrance is available in many shapes, forms, and sizes and obtainable in an array of scents. A scented candle or an unusual container of potpourri can be exciting as well as useful, and is a gift that is not usually purchased for oneself. A gift of fragrance wrapped creatively with a ribbon or raffia, tissue, or cello wrap and decorated with a sprig of fresh herbs, a charm, or a fresh flower, is a thoughtful statement that says thank you in a special way and can be enjoyed for a long time. A gift of fragrance presented in a crystal bowl or on a silver tray, can be a gift of elegance. When this type of gift is a scented candle, it is not only a gift of fragrance, it is illumination—like the moonlight of the night sky. Special touches will give your gift a personal kiss and the continuing fragrance will be a reminder of the emotion and feelings that were behind the gift.

What if the creative thing is just not you? Fine, then it's time for a shopping adventure.

Search for a usable souvenir from the vacation site you are visiting—make sure that it is usable and practical. We all have a drawer full of little *tchotchkes* that have no use. A useful souvenir-style thank you gift will let people know that you were thinking of them while you were away and, most importantly, that you wanted to do something special for them.

All of the above are easy and fun suggestions and can all be offered as simple gifts of appreciation. Always remember the number one rule: whatever gift you select, no matter how large or small, no matter if it is homemade or purchased, and no matter the cost, the gift must always be personally selected by you and given from your heart. The gift you select is a gesture or a token of appreciation, to someone who has extended a courtesy or favor on your behalf, that simply says thank you.

A Thank You for an Action Received

If you take a few moments to look back and review the day, you will probably find that courtesies or favors are received regularly, whether unexpected or upon request. Such courtesies or favors are what I like to call neighborly or friendly courtesies.

Neighborly or friendly courtesies can be as simple as bringing in the mail or newspaper in one's absence. They can be carpooling the kids to school or to sporting events or watering the lawn or flowers while someone is on vacation.

Taking the neighborly or friendly courtesies to the next step could be feeding the family pet when an afternoon meeting runs past the pet's dinnertime, making sure that little Bruiser's eating schedule is not interrupted. Perhaps they might offer to take little Bruiser for his evening walk.

We all go on vacations or out of town on trips, whether it be for pleasure or professional purposes, and we all know that it is a good idea to have someone watching over the old home front in our absence to pick up the newspaper or bring the mail in. Signs of an unoccupied house, such as an overstuffed mailbox or newspapers piled high in the driveway, are an open invitation for Harold Home Intruder to come on in and help himself to the family's valuables—usually unnoticed. The solution to this dilemma would be to call on a neighbor to keep an eye on your home in your absence. Whether living on a cul-de-sac or a maple tree-lined street in the suburbs, in a tower apartment in Manhattan, in a cabin tucked away in the mountains of Aspen, or on the beach in Malibu, we all have neighbors, and we are all faced with the out-of-town dilemma at one time or another. And most of our neighbors will face the same dilemma some time too. The out-of-town dilemma can be solved in a reciprocal fashion; it goes without saying that your neighbor would be more than willing to keep an eye on the happenings of the neighborhood while you are away since when your neighbor is out of town, you can reciprocate.

This type of neighborly courtesy usually does not involve hours upon hours of scheduled duties; the duties are limited and will only take a few minutes each day. These simple duties could be picking up the mail from the mail box or bringing in the newspaper. If you have a yard, the neighborly courtesy may include giving the lawn and possibly the plants a drink of water or making sure that the automatic sprinkler system is turning on and off properly. None of these courtesies would take a great deal of time, but they cannot be done when you are not home unless you call on a neighbor to take care of things for you. When you return from the trip and are picking up the house key, a small token of appreciation is a proper and considerate gesture, offering to the person who has been the gatekeeper in your absence a sincere thank you.

A small souvenir from the vacation location, a plate of baked goodies, a basket of fresh fruit or vegetables or a bouquet of fresh flowers from the garden, are all great expressions of how much you appreciate the kindness offered in your absence.

No rules or guidelines on what or how much the token should be; this is all up to you. Always enclose a handwritten thank you note.

Another example of a neighborly or friendly courtesy could be a schoolmate picking up your homework because you are feeling under the weather. And perhaps when the schoolmate drops off the homework at your house, he or she sticks around for a little while, to explain the lessons to you, making sure that you understand.

One neighborly or friendly courtesy that is often ignored is the simple courtesy of continued support by being there—in good times and in bad—to listen and to lend a shoulder to a person. The support from a special person who can always be counted on, through thick and thin; to talk to and share with. All of these actions are gifts from the heart, given to you and your family, by a friend, the neighbor next door, or an office associate. All of these acts of kindness and support are neighborly or friendly courtesies, and all are perfect occasions to take a moment and say thank you with a small gift and, of course, a handwritten note. Just a little something, given from you to a friend or neighbor, letting him or her know that you appreciate them for what they did for you, for who they are, and for how their kind act has enriched your life and touched your heart.

A Thank You in Appreciation

It is proper etiquette and a gesture of good manners, to offer a token in appreciation of something offered to you or a family member. A thank you in appreciation simply says that you, as the receiver, did notice and appreciate the favor or courtesy offered on your behalf. The teacher at your child's school gave extra help in math for several nights after school to ensure that your child moved up to the next grade level; the teenager living across the street came over and played with the kids while you studied for an exam required by work; a friend dropped by and helped with the cookie bake sale—all are favors, uninvited, that would qualify for a thank you in appreciation.

Flowers, candles, or even a lovely card with a personal note inside, express how much you appreciate the kindness or assistance that was extended to you or a family member. You might have lunch together, just to say thank you. A little something special to someone special can make all their time and hard work worthwhile.

SOMETHING FOR THE HOST/HOSTESS

When you are invited to someone's home for a meal or a gathering, a holiday celebration, or a summer dip in the swimming pool, a small token in appreciation for the invitation is a wonderful opportunity to say "thank you for sharing your home." It is a time that a small gift in appreciation is socially suggested and also suggested by proper etiquette, which, as we all know, represents good manners and is the proper thing to do.

A nice bottle of fine wine, a basket of chocolate chip cookies, a plate of brownies, a scented candle, or a box of chocolate truffles may be the perfect gift and may be incorporated into the menu planned for the gathering, or saved for the family's enjoyment at a later date. A potted plant, blooming tree, or a lush bush that can be placed on the patio; a bouquet of fresh flowers; or a serving dish or tray are just a few suggestions for the host/hostess. A jar of homemade jam is also a perfect gift. All are affordably priced and perfect gifts for the host/hostess that say thank you for sharing your home and your time.

Looking back on the many invitations that you have received over the years, how are you on this one? Did you remember to bring a small gift for your host/hostesses in appreciation of them sharing their home with you? Perhaps, in the past, applying this rule of social etiquette and good manners was not number one on your list. But now, there can be no excuse. The door on this rule has been opened; so in the future, give this social etiquette suggestion a try. It is a great opportunity to treat the host/hostess, as well as yourself, by sharing good feelings and a gift in appreciation, and it is the socially proper thing to do.

A host/hostess gift opportunity is not limited to sharing an invitation to one's home for a dinner or gathering. Another common opportunity is when someone is kind enough to host a celebration in your honor. Perhaps you are getting married and a wedding shower is in order, or you are expecting your first baby and a baby shower is planned; upon arrival to the celebration, it is always proper to honor the host/hostess with a gift. You may be starting a new business, maybe a business that is based around the selling of products through home parties, and a friend or neighbor has offered to host a party to kick-start the new venture in a most successful manner. Oftentimes, we are at a loss when a good friend or family member opens their home and offers to host an event, and we are sitting in the honor seat. The host or hostess is certainly not expecting anything for this kindness, which makes giving a hostess gift so much fun. Proper etiquette and simple grace states that a host and hostess should be recognized with a thank you for their kindness and hard work in honor of a courtesy extended on your behalf. And a proper, suggested form of recognition is a token of appreciation.

Chocolates arranged in a candy dish or basket, antique or purchased in accordance to the personal taste of the host/hostess, wrapped with cello wrap and tied with a lovely ribbon—decadent!

Scented candles presented in a similar wrap or tissue, placed in a gift bag, in a holder, or beautiful container, or simply tied with a ribbon—fragrant, romantic, and definitely says love!

A unique box, creatively filled with the host's/hostess's favorite hard candies, stationery, or miniature candles—elegant and yummy!

A vase, china or etched glass, filled with flowers of color and sunshine that can be placed in the kitchen window or on an entry table—beautiful!

One important note on the gift of flowers: it is wise to make a flower selection with the vision of placement somewhere other than the dining table as a centerpiece, as you certainly do not wish this bouquet of beauty to clash with the china or planed décor of the evening.

A basket of fresh fruits or vegetables, creatively arranged and finished with a recipe that is a family favorite—personal and from the heart!

Soaps, bath oils, and lotions, along with a few decorative hand towels, personally selected for the host's/hostess's home—useful, yet lovely!

A gift for a manicure and/or pedicure, a facial, or makeup services, offered by a professional artist, even a body massage or herbal wrap; all are wonderful and relaxing!

Selecting the perfect gift for the host/hostess may have been difficult in the past, but now, the possibilities are unlimited. You may wish to move in the direction of a more personal gift, a piece of clothing to wear or a fun bag to carry, which can definitely say this was selected just for you. And if a decision still cannot be made, perhaps a gift certificate would be the path to travel.

A host/hostess gift is simply a small gesture that says how much you appreciate the kind and thoughtful gift that was given to you by his or her hosting a very special event in your honor.

WELCOME TO OUR NEIGHBORHOOD

Here is a neighborly occasion where is it socially suggested to give a gift, a small gift that says welcome to a new neighbor who has just moved into the neighborhood—an occasion that some people do not think of.

In the past twenty years, our family has lived in the same house, in the same neighborhood, in the same city in sunny California. As we all know, California is considered the melting pot of the United States with thousands of families and individuals moving in and out of the state, 24/7. Going back as far as the days of the California gold rush, thousands of people have poured into this beautiful melting pot, to find their fortunes, to establish new businesses in the land of opportunity, or to find their fame in Hollywood.

Our family just loves the sun, the beaches, and the wonderful mix of people; and, of course, this state just happened to be where my husband was employed. When we were house hunting, the family made a promise that our perfect new home would include a very large backyard, would have space between our home and the home next door, and would be located away from the busy streets. And, *bingo*, we hit the jackpot! We were able to fill the bill on a cozy cul-de-sac we now call our home. Our particular neighborhood is presently home to a total of thirteen families, four of which have been occupied by the original families since their building date, leaving nine of the homes having been sold and resold in the past twenty years. Each and every time a new family moves into the neighborhood, all of the families on the block come together to greet the newcomers with welcome goodies. Gifts usually are baked or planted in a pot and growing, but without fail, we all make the journey to the front door of the new neighbor's home with a gift in hand to say hello and welcome to the neighborhood.

It is rare that the newcomer will know anyone on the block in a new neighborhood, so a welcome gift is a nice way to introduce yourself and say hello to another family—and another pair of eyes that may be available to partake in the neighborhood watch, another family that can be available to talk to, or another family to exchange a wave back and forth with at the end of a busy day. Your gift most likely will be welcome, as who feels like baking or making a market run when you first move into a new house?

A PROFESSIONAL THANK YOU

A professional thank you gift, or token of appreciation, can be a touchy and somewhat tricky subject, especially in an office or professional setting where there are many people working together in one space. Let's begin by saying that when you decide it is the appropriate time to acknowledge a coworker, an associate, an employee/employer, or other business-related acquaintance by giving a gift, it is strongly suggested that you choose the time and the place carefully so the gift will not appear to be a gift of favoritism. Favoritism is not received warmly by fellow coworkers, by associates, or by employees/employers in a professional setting.

When the time and the place are both right, and you are a professional who works closely with vendors or colleagues and the advice or referrals from these associates have helped create the success of your business, it may be the time for a professional thank you gift. When a particular person or persons within the structure of your business have taken that extra step or gone beyond the call of duty on the behalf of the business, it may be time for a professional thank you gift. Perhaps the decision of giving a gift is based on loyalty or respect for an associate, coworker, or employee in honor of actions extended on behalf of the company or toward fellow employees, and you want this person to know that you appreciate and have noticed the extra efforts and actions given to you, to fellow coworkers, or to the business on your behalf. The rule of thumb on professional thank you gifts is before you make the first move, confirm with company policy that a gift of any kind is acceptable in your specific work place. If it is acceptable, the gates are open, and you are on your way.

All of these examples are perfect opportunities to give a gift of thanks, but the time and the place are essential. The appropriate time, the proper place, and, of course, the perfect selection of the token of appreciation must be handled professionally and, most of all, must always be determined by you.

Perhaps a one-to-one token of appreciation could be in a meal form. Breakfast, lunch, or dinner for two could be enjoyed by the honored person and a guest of his or her choice. This type of gift would be an appropriate professional thank you.

It is also wise that when this type of gift of appreciation is presented, it is done in a gift certificate form, never cash, and that the choice of presentation be in an envelope, a wrapped and ribbon-tied box, or in some other concealed manner. Always keep in mind that the other people in the same space are all very eager to see what the boss is doing. Other possible suggestions may be a nice meal shared with the boss. This, too, can be a proper and appropriate professional gift.

Flowers, an arrangement of candles, a box of candy, or a nice wine or champagne by the bottle or a case arranged in a basket, are all wonderful professional gifts as well.

A specialty folder, calendar, or pen, personalized by engraving a name and date of meaning, can be added to the list of perfect professional gifts.

A token of appreciation not only confirms to your colleagues that they are appreciated, but also that their efforts have not gone unnoticed. A token of appreciation is the package, arranged in a basket or wrapped and crowned with a beautiful ribbon. And the completion of the perfect package is a handwritten note or enclosure, which is the ultimate expression that the gift is sincere, filled with forethought, and was personally selected by you.

Time for a reality check; let's get serious here. How many of us have a boss or are bosses who actually take the time or have the time to personally shop for a gift? Answer? Not many. But even though the actual gift may have been sent, made, or picked out by someone else, there are no rules that say the thank you note should to be in a stranger's handwriting or preprinted in a generic form. A personally handwritten enclosure will enhance any gift, and there is always time to do it! You ask, "How can a handwritten note be enclosed in a gift that is ordered or has been sent from an outside source?" *Piece of cake*, I answer, with confidence and the perfect solution: if the gift is sent on your behalf from a florist, gift or department store, or vineyard or winery, an actual handwritten note or enclosure can be delivered or mailed to the origin of the gift. All you have to do is write the note and send it off or have it delivered prior to the delivery of the gift. Include instructions that your handwritten thank you note be enclosed with the gift to be delivered to that very special person. Problem solved!

When the gift you have selected is packed up for mailing or delivery to that special someone, your handwritten note, including your personal expressions and finished with your personal signature, completes the package. This handwritten thank you is then placed carefully in the package, as if you were standing at the counter of the store or vendor's shop that the special gift was selected from, with pen and stationery in hand, waiting to enclose your personal and very special thank you note. The actual handwriting is an important personal touch that may take a few moments longer, but in the end, will mean so much when the gift is received.

On your next professional occasion, when a little token would be appropriate, try it—you'll no doubt have an unbelievable result!

In Celebration of a Special Event or Day

Giving a gift for a special occasion or on a special day is one of the easiest time to give a gift, one that has been practiced throughout every year of our lives, beginning at a very early age; we all have the basics rules and guidelines down reasonably well, don't we?

The rule of proper etiquette states that it is always proper to give a gift to the honored guest for birthdays, weddings, baby or bridal showers, graduations, baptisms, mitzvahs, monumental promotions, and, of course, for holidays such as Hanukkah and Christmas. Like any gift, the cost or creativity of the gift is entirely up to you. On some occasions, it may be the tradition or custom to give a monetary gift; again, the amount of the gift and the manner of presentation—wrapped, packaged, or tucked in an envelope or card—is up to you as the giver.

When you are invited to a celebration, you bring a gift for the person you are celebrating, the guest of honor. Often you can figure out a perfect and appropriate gift for the occasion all by yourself as it is not usually a difficult task to undertake. But if you do run into a wall trying to decide on that perfect gift, the solution is as easy as making a telephone phone call to a family member of the honored guest, or a close friend who is also an invited guest attending the celebration; the suggestions and ideas will begin to pour in like running water from a tap, and the rest is up to you.

When the decision is made and the perfect gift is in your hands, wrap or bag the gift and attach a personally hand-signed card to the package, then you are on your way.

Just imagine. You are invited to a birthday party, and as you enter the party, a parent or family friend takes the gift from your hands and places the gift on a table, a massive table piled high with tons of other gifts. Suddenly, your eyes widen like saucers and the light turns on in your brain as you remember: there is no card on the gift!

What do you do? You are certainly bright enough to know that going up to the birthday person and whispering in his ear that your gift is "the one with no card" is not the solution. First, your message will probably not be heard due to the excitement of the party. Second, the chance of the birthday person remembering what you said is one in a million—your whispered words would probably go in one ear and out the other. And third, there is always the possibility that there will be other gifts with no card piled on that same massive table.

So what do you do? At that point, there is nothing you can do. You will just have to wait until the present is opened, then you can speak up and announce that you were the one who forgot to attach a gift card. But, next time, there is an easy foolproof answer: never forget to attach a gift card to the present—never!

And the moral of this story? A gift card not only personalizes the gift for the receiver and is a perfect time to write a few personal words to the guest of honor, but it also identifies the giver of the gift, alleviating total chaos and confusion at gift-opening time. A gift card is one of those must-do things when presenting any gift at any time. The lesson to be learned from this story is that if you are willing to put forth the effort in getting a gift for an occasion and in arriving at the celebration on time, you may as well put forth a little more effort and attach a gift card to any gift that you present.

Three steps:
- First, get the gift.
- Second, attach the card to the gift.
- Third, arrive at the celebration on time.

Three very easy steps with one additional suggestion: take the second step to the next level by writing a personal little note inside the celebration or gift card. What a nice idea—two gifts in one. A note that is personal and from the heart, and a sure guarantee that whatever gift you have selected, will be identified as a gift from you; a gift that was purchased with care, and a gift from your heart.

In Remembrance

We all are painfully aware of the fact that where there is a beginning, there is also an ending—similar to the chapters of a good novel, the story line of a great movie, or birth and death; it is a hard fact of life that we all experience. And during those times of loss or endings, a simple reminder from those we love can be a warm comfort, can make the tears seem lighter, and can help the sunshine come through the clouds on a otherwise rainy day, giving hope that there will be an end to the sorrow. Most all of us know that a basket, a container of fresh flowers, or a potted plant, sent to a final resting place in remembrance of one who has passed, is often a suitable gift in remembrance—a socially expected gesture in honor and respect of someone who has passed and for those who are left behind.

But did you know that it is also appropriate to offer personal services? An offer to prepare or bring food to the location of the reception that will follow the ceremony or to the home of the family member who is traveling down this road of personal loss is a thoughtful and compassionate gesture, either prior to the services or within a respectable amount of time following the loss.

It is also appropriate to offer assistance for the needs at hand. To pick up the kids from school or to pick up items that have been ordered for the reception that follows the service can be a much-needed gift.

An offer to be available for the setup and cleanup of the reception would be most appreciated. An offer to stay behind during the services can ensure that all of the reception details will be honored and everything will be set in its proper place. With the follow-through of the reception arrangements taken care of, when the family and friends gather together, every detail will be ready to welcome the guests.

Some feel that this type of offer or gesture might be taken as an imposition, however, that is rarely the case. These gestures of courtesy, kindness, and thoughtfulness are taken as gifts, special gifts that are often overlooked at this very difficult time, as it may be awkward to ask such a favor of friends or family, even though the need is present and the offer would be most welcome. At a time of loss, it is comforting to have family and friends around, who we love and who we are loved by, supporting us in many ways. Unfortunately, the loss of a family member or a close friend is a situation that is part of life; the comfort of family and friends is always welcome.

Where there is a beginning or birth, there will also be an ending or death, a situation that we all will experience at both ends of the story, and a situation where we can let our friends know how wonderful and comforting it is to stand by their side, letting them know that they are not alone. To know we can depend on those around us in good times and in bad times in unconditional friendship, is both treasured and appreciated.

A gift of remembrance may be offered when we do not personally know the person who has passed, but do know and love the spouse, daughter, son, or sibling who is left behind. Personal support is a way to soften the burden and wipe away a few tears, and to let survivors know that we are thinking of them and are offering help and assist in their time of loss.

A small gift of flowers that bring sunshine and joy—a living plant—can symbolize life eternal. A book or poem written by you or published by an author who you both love and enjoy, personally sent or delivered to the one who is close to you, can bring comfort to the heart and serve as a reminder that you are there at their time of loss. And the offers of assistance in any way are all gifts of remembrance and gifts that say you care.

All gifts of remembrance are appreciated and simply state that someone's loss is felt and will be honored by you through the bond you share. When there are miles between you, a simple card or a poem can serve as an important token at this time of sorrow—a message that can be revisited as the days go by and the pain of the loss is still vivid in their hearts, a gift of remembrance directly from your heart to a friend.

When reading this chapter, look back into your mind, then leap forward into the future, and you will be reminded of all of the many, wonderful opportunities you have to say thank you to your friends, your family, your neighbors, and your coworkers. While you are taking this journey through your past and into the future, you can also be reminded of how special one feels when someone you have been kind to acknowledges that kindness with a thank you of any kind. During this journey, you will also be reminded how wonderful it feels when you have the opportunity to reciprocate a kindness with a thank you. These are moments that you will file in your memory bank that are filled with meaningful lessons that can be revisited time and time again. And each time the journey is made, you can again experience that warm and fuzzy feeling, that complete feeling of love and comfort that engulfs your entire body when you have taken the time to extend a thank you to someone who is special in your life.

Chapter Eight
Gratuities and Tips

THIS IS AN important topic, a real social puzzler and one that most people do not have a clue about when asked the ongoing questions about.

When is it appropriate to give a gratuity or tip?

And, how much should it be?

The first step in understanding a word is to discover its meaning, and the meaning of the word *gratuity*, simply stated, is a monetary thank you for a job well-done. In lieu of what many people may believe, a gratuity is not a service charge, nor a charge for food or beverage. Service charges are separate and completely different in meaning, especially when working with contracted vendors on a special event where they are most often included in the final bill. A gratuity is seldom included in a service contract.

A gratuity is a monetary thank you for a service offered or rendered by an employee of an establishment for a service you have contracted for or purchased. It is a gift of gratitude in a monetary form given directly to the individual who has offered or performed a service or talent on your behalf. Wow, that was a bit wordy, but I am confident that you got the drift of it.

Gratuities can be placed in two different etiquette categories: *Social* and *Proper*, and many of us have problems determining the difference between the two. Let me make this easier for you. A social gratuity is an expected gratuity, outlined by society dating back to the early 1900s and directed by the rules of etiquette, for a service rendered; the amount or percentage of the gratuity in most cases will be outlined for you. The gratuity amount is the base suggested amount that is given to anyone who has offered a service; an expected set amount to be given by the engager of the service to the provider of that service.

A proper gratuity is based on good common sense which represents an acknowledgment that the service rendered to you is appreciated. However, there is more to it. In today's world we have all seen many changes with regard to services rendered, and there are varied opinions on the proper gratuity that should be given in appreciation of that service. When understood, determining the proper amount is easy. If a service rendered is above and beyond the call of duty, good common sense extends the option of adding to the social base amount depending on the level of service rendered. If the service rendered is less then desirable, the social base amount is given. Never is a service rendered without an offer of appreciation in gratuity form.

In looking back at the many events that I have produced over the years, one of the most commonly asked questions is regarding gratuity. A gratuity is one of the most appreciated and gratifying gifts that can be bestowed on any contracted vendor, for without their talent and participation, an event would not be a success. A gratuity may be placed in a little envelope and presented at the end of an evening, along with a smile and those magic words of thank you, which may go something like, "Because of you, this evening was a great success. Thank you for making my dreams come true."

For a vendor, being told that their participation on your special day made a difference is like a pot of gold at the end of a rainbow. Not only is it socially expected to extend a gratuity along with a few words of appreciation, it is also the proper thing to do. A true double-hitter!

In the following pages, you will begin to learn the differences between the two types of gratuities. You will be able to determine when and how to respond to both gratuity situations. You will also learn the similarities between the two gratuities, social and proper, and will understand why both are considered a thank you for a service rendered or a job well-done. You will understand why it is so important that both are acknowledged by you to the service person, with a smile followed by saying the magic words, thank you.

During the orchestration of any event with my clients, we always visit the gratuity issue. It is a sure thing that the question will come up, and if not, it would be brought to the table by me. Who should a gratuity be presented or given to, and what is an appropriate amount to give to each of the many service people who have been contracted for an event?

As we all know, the planning of a perfect party takes time, and as the end of the orchestration approaches, usually two weeks from the event date, a written list of balances due and a notation regarding a suggested gratuity to each vendor is given to my clients. I also make suggestions as to how the gratuity should be presented. On the top of the suggestion list is always the statement that a gratuity should be presented by the giver of the gift; that is what makes it so special. I would also suggest that a thank you note, handwritten and signed by the client, be placed in an envelope with the monetary gratuity, magically turning this gift of appreciation from pewter to platinum.

Traveling through the chapters of this book and reaching back into our memory banks, we all have learned that being consistent with any task we undertake makes our actions proper without thought, and with practice, those actions become perfect. In a nutshell, with practice, our actions will become the best that they can be.

A tip is also a monetary thank you, in cash or check form, therefore, the word tip has the same meaning as the word gratuity. When referring to the dictionary, the definition of the word *gratuity* uses *grateful* and *gratitude*. When referring to the dictionary for the word *tip*, it reads *money*; a bit crude, but certainly to the point. So when we think of giving a gratuity or tip, in 99.9 percent of the situations, think thank you in a monetary form. There are numerous occasions where a gratuity is appropriate and it would probably be impossible to cover each and every one of the occasions, whether the gratuity is suggested by society or by proper etiquette; however, let's give it a try, shall we?

In a personal situation, when we say thank you to a friend or family member for a service or favor received, we do it with a gift or note of our choice. We, of course, do not usually tip or present a gratuity to our friends or family on a personal basis. We do, however, offer a gratuity or tip if the friend or family member has been contracted to perform a specific talent or service as if they were a contracted vendor. If this is the situation, a contract for service or talent, whether friend, family member, or perfect stranger, is considered to be a business deal, not a personal deal, and we should treat the business deal accordingly. That way, no one will ever feel as if they are being taken advantage of. There is a very fine line between personal and professional when it comes to business, and in consideration of that line, it is always better to look at the favor professionally, rather than personally. At least make the offer, and if rejected, no problem! You did offer a token of appreciation as you would to any other contracted vendor indicating to your talented friends or family members that their services were valuable and appreciated.

Rule Number One: When working with service people, following a service rendered, offer a gratuity or tip in a monetary form—always! This is a simple rule, motivated by common sense, and outlined by either social or proper etiquette based on the situation, and this rule is not up for debate!

When giving a social gratuity, there is a suggested monetary amount or percentage that is expected and outlined by society as a gratuity or tip. And for a proper etiquette gratuity, most often, the choice is up to you, with a few exceptions. Because a proper gratuity is motivated by common sense and not by a socially outlined suggested amount, when confronted with the question of a proper gratuity, take a moment and think about it. Reach back into your memory bank and ask the question, "Is offering a gratuity the proper thing to do?" Chances are more likely than not, that common sense will always answer yes. Therefore a gratuity is appropriate.

We all know that when we go to a restaurant, we are expected to leave a gratuity or tip, making a restaurant visit a perfect example of a social gratuity. But did you know that it is also appropriate to offer a gratuity or tip to the bagging person when we go to the market for a big shopping purchase? Yes, this would be a proper gratuity. Or did you know that when you have the car washed and cleaned, it is suggested that a gratuity is offered to the attendant(s) who have rendered the service? Again, yes, this is another example of a proper gratuity. How about when you pull into a hotel or resort and a valet opens your car door, parks your car, and then brings your car back to you upon presentation of your valet ticket when you depart? Yes, this situation would be a social gratuity. When you walk through the doors of the hotel and a door person is kind enough to open the door as you enter? When the bell person brings your luggage to your room after you check in or assists in bringing your luggage back down to your car when you check out? Yes, yes. A tip for the door person would be a proper gratuity, and as for the bell person, most definitely an expected social gratuity.

Whether a gratuity is a gift outlined socially or by proper etiquette, these are all perfect examples of a time for you to reach into your pocket and say thank you.

Let's take a few more moments (or shall I say pages), and revisit all of the above opportunities, one by one, that are directed either by social or proper etiquette, suggesting when it is appropriate to reach into your pocket and give a gratuity or tip as a token of your appreciation for a service rendered or a job well-done.

AT THE MARKET

When you go to the grocery market with that long list of food and supplies that must be purchased to fill your cupboards, your freezer, and your fridge, and there is a person at the end of the check-out counter who is bagging up your groceries in paper or plastic, and then puts all of the bags of groceries in your cart, pushes the cart or carts out to your car, and then places all of those bags, one by one into your car. Question time. Is this an appropriate time to offer a gratuity? Yes, this is a proper gratuity or tip time. A service has been extended to you by an employee of an establishment, correct? You are grateful for the assistance, as you certainly had no intention of doing all that work by yourself. So, the proper thing to do, or the proper etiquette thing to do, would be to offer this assistant a gratuity or a tip. Perhaps a few dollars placed in the palm of his or her hand, never forgetting that big smile and those magic words, thank you. There is one point of information that must be shared on this subject. Some markets, usually big chain corporations, suggest that the employees are not permitted, by company policy, to take a monetary gratuity. This policy should be explained to you upon offering the gift, and if that is the case, perfect! You will understand, but either way, you made the offer, which says to the service person that you do appreciate the efforts extended to you. You then seal the deal with a smile and a few words of thanks. We all love to be appreciated and recognized for our efforts and, for that matter, we all love a helping hand offered by employees at markets, home-fix-it stores and garden centers, especially when our carts are filled to the brim. Just keep in mind, when dealing with service people—and people in general—the old and wise saying that should be remembered and put into play: *"what goes around, comes around."* You enjoy it when your efforts are appreciated, and just like you, everyone else likes to be appreciated too. A warm and sincere gesture of appreciation is the reward that we all enjoy from one time to another. When an opportunity arises and you are questioning the situation as to whether or not a gratuity or tip should be offered, put yourself on the other side of the court—flip the deal. I can assure you that more often than not, the offer of a gratuity or tip will be appropriate to put into motion. A few dollars certainly will not break the bank, and a smile along with those two little magic words, "thank you," will make you feel like a million dollars when extended to a person who has gone the extra mile on your behalf. And, in turn, that million-dollar feeling will double as the person who has accepted the gratuity will share by the expression on his or her face just how happy they were to assist you. Try it! It is a win-win situation.

Out to Eat

Alright, now you are in a restaurant, the wait staff has greeted you, served your beverage, and offered assistance with the menu by answering the many questions you may have. Then, in a timely manner, the server has taken your menu order and has served the order to you and to the members of your party. At the end of your meal, when your check is presented, you are socially expected to include a monetary gratuity for the service rendered. In review: A server from the establishment has extended a service to you and, in turn, you say thank you to this person with a gratuity or tip. At a restaurant, a gratuity or tip is a socially expected rule. There really is no question as to whether or not a gratuity should be left at a restaurant—the answer is always yes. This is a perfect example of a social gratuity and should always be included at the end of each meal served in a restaurant or eating establishment. Leaving a gratuity is another one of those silent rules that we all must obey according to the guidelines of social etiquette.

The gratuity is a percentage of the charge for the food and beverage; not including sales tax. Relax, Uncle Sam will always receive his cut in a timely manner.

Here is an interesting fact that many are probably not aware of: In the state of California, you are expected to leave a 15 percent gratuity for the server at a restaurant for just receiving the meal. This is true. It doesn't really matter how great the service or food was, you leave a minimum of 15 percent of the check before tax, just because you were served. Of course, if the service and the food were amazing, as a patron of the establishment you have the option to leave a greater percentage for the gratuity; 20 is a very comfortable and common California percentage for a gratuity following a meal; it's easy to figure out and most definitely appreciated when received by your server.

In other states across our grand and wonderful nation, there is no set percentage suggested as a gratuity, but just because the amount is not preset for you, you are not off the hook. At the end of the meal, when your check is presented to you, always leave a gratuity for the server; this social gratuity rule still applies. Begin at 10 percent of the check amount before the tax and work your way up from there. Base your decision on the level of service you received, the quality of the food, and the region you are in, and you know what? It is a given that you will determine the perfect amount for the gratuity. Always bear in mind that any reasonable gratuity is not hard to calculate and, most importantly, will be appreciated by the server.

Another interesting fact is that in some restaurants, the management will add the gratuity, in the amount of 15–20 percent of the food less tax, directly onto the check before it is presented to the table. On occasion, this charge is called a service charge, informing the patrons of the establishment that the servers will be tipped automatically for their hard work. The words *service charge* at a restaurant are not to be confused with the same words used on a vendor contract or at a hotel or resort following a special event, as they are different.

The practice of adding on this charge at a restaurant is usually noted on the menu or posted on the premises, close to the sign that reads, "We reserve the right …" This add-on percentage for gratuity is usually enforced when serving groups larger than eight people in the same party. Is this legal? It certainly is, and it is also something that is expected—socially expected.

Fact: Larger groups in the same party are more difficult to serve and to take care of than a group of three or four guests.

Fact: Larger groups can also be more time-consuming for the server to attend to, leaving less time and fewer tables to serve during his or her shift, which might result in less accumulated tips for the evening.

So, if you are a part of a large group at a restaurant for a meal, be prepared to look over your charges carefully when you receive your check.

First, be sure to look at the bottom of your check before you automatically add on an additional percentage for the gratuity and place your credit card down on the table. The gratuity, as noted above, will sometimes be referred to as the service charge and may already be included in your final total.

Again, as the patron, you have the option, based on the service received and the quality and presentation of the food that was consumed, to leave a larger tip, above the stated percentage for gratuity.

Be aware that there is a flip side to this practice. Possibly the restaurant you visit may not practice the larger group tip policy and may not automatically add on a charge for serving a larger group; please do not assume that the gratuity has already been considered. If there is not a gratuity or service charge noted on the bottom of the check, it is up to you to leave a gratuity. No, your large group is not getting a break because it was so delightful to take care of all of you—nice try. If the gratuity has not visibly been added into your total, you will need to figure out a proper percentage to be included in your final check. Revisit the service and the food, and begin your decision by leaving a minimum of 15 percent of the food and beverage total without tax, whether you are in California or any other state. An 18 percent gratuity would be the suggested base for service rendered to a larger group based on the extra time and effort that has been extended.

Keep in mind that because a social gratuity is expected at the end of a meal, and in most cases a suggested percentage is outlined for you, you may apply the rule of the proper gratuity, which says that when the service is very good, you as the patron have the option to leave whatever you wish above the expected percentage as your thank you for a service well-done. The additional amount is, of course, up to you. A gratuity is a monetary thank you for the service and assistance rendered to the people around your table during a meal. I feel that we can all agree that being a server or waiter/waitress is very hard work. Reach back into your memory bank and refer to the old and wise saying noted earlier, and when you go out for a meal and when you leave your thank you gratuity, make sure that the gratuity represents something that you personally would feel good about receiving. And when the opportunity comes up again for you to return to the restaurant, believe me, the servers will remember you and your generosity—and quite possibly even remember your favorite salad dressing.

One fact that is not commonly known is that at some restaurants, the gratuities are the salary or the biggest portion of the salary for the servers. Somewhat shocking, but true! The servers may not be working for an hourly rate during their shift, and if there is an hourly rate, it is most likely at minimum wage or even less. Therefore, if the servers do not receive gratuities or tips, there is no bread on their tables, so to speak. The gratuities received by the servers during their scheduled shifts, may be the greater portion of their salaries and something that they depend on just like a full-time employee at a financial institution depends on a monthly paycheck. And just like the employee in a large corporation, you can be assured that this form of salary is also a salary that Uncle Sam receives taxes on, usually on a quarterly basis. When the gratuity form of salary is overlooked by the patrons who are served by service personnel, this oversight can be like losing a month's rent.

I have actually seen large and small groups of restaurant guests leave only the meal charges on the table and then depart from the restaurant—no tip or gratuity, just payment for the food check and nothing else. To a server, this is like a slap in the face with a nice piece of halibut, cold and thoughtless!

Here is my unsolicited opinion on the subject, and I sincerely feel that we are all on the same side of the fence on this one. Waiting tables and attending to the public's needs, especially when the people are hungry, can have its good points and its bad points, but bottom line is that it is a very hard job! No, I am not nor have I ever been a waitress or server, but over many years of experience in the service business, at events and personally, I feel that I have seen my fair share of situations. I can strongly say, with deep respect and full support, that I appreciate all of the hard work and stress, not to mention the juggling acts that most servers are expected to perform. I will also say that I personally would not have the patience or stamina for the job, so kudos and many thanks to you all, for your participation in making my events run smoothly and for making my personal out-of-home experiences so enjoyable. Hopefully, the majority of patrons that you deal with during a scheduled shift will be delightful to serve and will acknowledge and honor the etiquette rules mapped out by society and simple good manners regarding a thank you gratuity.

Here is another situation with regard to a gratuity at a restaurant or while enjoying a meal outside the comfort of your own home. Let's say that the server is a friend or relative of your family—a struggling student, someone you care about for whom this is his or her first job, or an associate who has fallen on hard times and is waiting tables for extra living expenses—and he or she has done a nice job of taking care of all of your needs throughout the course of your meal. You, as the patron, again have the choice of leaving a gratuity in any amount you wish. Remember, if you are in California, the gratuity that is left begins at 15 percent before tax. If you are in another state, the base percentage begins at 10 percent before tax. These percentages are the socially expected and suggested percentages for a gratuity, and anything over and above that amount is up to you. Always remember that a big smile and the magic words, thank you, two small and free actions extended by you, the patron, to the server, are like the whipped cream and cherries on top of an ice cream sundae and a perfect conclusion to a wonderful dining experience.

One additional comment with regards to a gratuity for your meal, and my final "did-you-know?" fact on this subject. At many restaurants, the gratuities are placed in a pool or pot and combined with all of the other gratuities that have been received during the scheduled shift by all the staff. Then, at the end of the shift, all of the gratuities are divided between the servers, bus personnel, and sometimes even the kitchen staff. So please don't be too conservative with the gratuity gift. There is a chance that that gratuity will be divided among a number of people at the end of the day; you can be assured that there was definitely more than one person responsible for your meal and the enjoyable time that you experienced. End result: more than one person will experience and share your appreciation that is extended by the gratuity included in the check, so make the gratuity a comfortable and fair gift—another one of those win-win situations.

AT THE CAR WASH

A car wash provides an opportunity for a proper gratuity for a service that is rendered on your behalf by the employee(s) of an establishment. Think about it!

Your car is filthy—so gross that the neighbor kids have left little messages in the built-up dirt that has settled on the paint job of your car, suggesting that in the very near future, a bath for this baby might be a good idea. On the inside of the car, spilled cola, chocolate milk, or coffee have created mysterious patterns, transforming that once nice, fluffy texture of the carpet into a matted and flat hard surface, a surface that may see muddy soccer cleats that would be more welcome on the doormat on your back porch. The animal crackers and pretzels crushed between the seats and scattered all over the floor present the question: what color is the carpet anyway? Is it really soft gray?

And that chili dog that you didn't quite finish over a week ago that was tossed on the floor behind you, leaving the less than desirable fragrance now permeating throughout the interior of your car? Honestly, do you really want to clean this mess up? Not on your life! So you go to the neighborhood car wash; you drive up, hand your keys to the attendant(s); and watch as they begin their magic while you enjoy a cup of your favorite java and catch up on your favorite magazine or the newspaper that you picked up on the doorstep as you left your house that morning.

Occasionally, you glance up to see if the messages once embedded in the dirt on the back of your car have been erased by the attendants hard at work.

Following the washing, wiping down, and polishing of the outside of the car—including those greasy hubcaps, rims, and tires—the attendants begin the task of shampooing the carpet and deodorizing the inside of your car. The result? After a long and hard workout, the attendants of the car wash have magically restored your "pride and joy" back into that car you remembered, leaving all of the dirt and messages, the food, drinks, and fragrances, and every bit of the unidentifiable stuff behind. The finished product is a sparkling clean car, as fresh as it was the day it was driven off the lot. Wow, who would have thought it possible?

Your next suggested proper etiquette move is to give the attendants a gratuity, correct? Absolutely! That was hard work, removing all of the dirt from the outside of your car, shoveling through the unidentifiable stuff that was stored all over the inside, getting rid of the smells, and then transforming that mini junkyard into something you can once again take pride in driving. Believe me, the hourly rate that the attendants are paid by their employer for this job will not come close to the level of satisfaction that you will experience after the job is done by the car wash attendants—plus, you were given an unexpected, irreplaceable gift: the gift of time. Time you used to sit down and relax for a while, an opportunity that is becoming more precious to each and every one of us in this very busy world.

As a thank you, reach into your pocket and start pulling out a few dollar bills! A good starting point for this proper etiquette gratuity occasion would be a minimum fifteen percent of the car cleaning charge. How much can that be? A 15 percent tip on a service that costs you maybe one Jackson bill is a whopping three bucks! The cup of java that you enjoyed while the service was being offered was more than that! So when that amount is established in your mind or on a piece of paper, revisit the service you received, relive the experience of relaxing while the attendants were taking care of your car, then make the adjustments to the amount of the gratuity in an upward direction. If the attendants really did go above and beyond the call of duty, dig a little deeper into your pocket for that thank you gratuity: maybe 20 percent or 25 percent, then hand the gratuity to the attendant(s) who worked so hard on your car—personally, from your hand to theirs. Don't forget those two little extras: a big smile and the magic words, thank you. When it is all said and done, your car will look just like new, and you didn't have to lift a finger; well, possibly one finger as you were flipping the pages of your favorite magazine. And in the future, when you pull in to the car wash, the attendants will greet you with big smiles, eager to once again do a great job for you because they will remember the kind acknowledgement for the hard work rendered with a gratuity in appreciation of a job well-done. Let's move on.

What About The Household Help?

You may have contracted with a personal gardener, pool maintenance service, housekeeper, window washer, or nanny. In many homes in this busy world, you will employ at least one of the above services, or maybe more than one. In a two-parent working home, it is very likely that you will have more than one of the above services contracted with to assist in making your home run more smoothly. The fact is, you are at work all day, and someone has to keep the weeds down in the yard and take care of the kids. For whatever reason service vendors are contracted with, an occasional gratuity can often times stimulate the continued good work from your service people and even encourage your workers to take the next step up in the service without even asking.

When service people are contracted for personal home service, often a holiday, such as Christmas or Hanukkah, is a nice time to offer a gratuity just to let them know that they are doing a good job and that you appreciate their service. A gift of appreciation on a high holiday, such as Easter or Passover, is also appropriate, so a little something on an occasion, such as the above holidays, would be a nice surprise. It can also serve as a subtle reminder that you expect a good job—without saying a word. A gratuity for a service person contracted with by you for your personal needs would be another one of those double-coined gratuities, outlined by both social and proper etiquette. The social rule says that the service personnel are most likely employed by an establishment or company and that the company service has been contracted with by you to perform a specific service on your behalf. The actual company or establishment will bill you, probably on a monthly basis, but the company or establishment assigns a service person to perform the actual job. A specific person is performing a service, correct? And you should recognize that person with a thank you, a thank you in gratuity form. Acknowledging your appreciation for the job he or she is doing is a nice thing to do, a proper thing to do, and the flip side of the double coin or a proper etiquette gratuity. If the gratuity is given at a less celebrated holiday, such as Valentine's Day or on someone's birthday, the suggested amount is really up to you. If it is given at a well-known holiday, such as Christmas or Hanukkah, the social rule says the gratuity amount could begin at 50 percent of one month of service.

Here is an example. You have a lovely yard that is mowed, planted, fed, and taken care of by a gardening service. The monthly charge from your gardener for these services is one hundred dollars per month. So, fifty dollars would be the suggested gratuity base or thank-you-gift-amount given to the gardener who actually mows the lawn, when a thank you gift is given at Christmas or Hanukkah showing your appreciation for a job well-done. It's that easy!

Remember that the monthly charges that have been contracted for a particular service rendered are for the service only. They are not the thank you gratuity given for a job well-done. The thank you gratuity is above the monthly charge or flat charge.

Some people feel that the gratuity is included in a flat rate, and this is rarely the case. And if on some rare occasion a gratuity is added to the monthly service bill, you can bet that the person who is actually performing the service will never see a penny of that amount. The key word here is service, and if you receive a service from a particular person, the door opens for a thank you—a thank you by giving a gratuity for that service, personally to the person who has rendered the service.

The above gratuity suggestion applies to anyone who offers assistance in making your life nicer and more enjoyable on a personal basis. Remember, persons contracted for manicures or pedicures, facials or massages, or a hair stylist or even a pet sitter. All of these services are offered by very important people in your life, people who make your day just a little bit brighter, and offering a thank you to these people with a gratuity is the right thing to do, a proper thing to do, and hence a proper gratuity. You may wish to honor a personal service person with something other than a monetary gratuity. A tangible gift can be a lovely acknowledgement, and as long as each time a personal service is rendered to you, a form of thank you is included, the etiquette rule is honored. Remember that smile and the magic words, thank you.

HOME DELIVERIES—TIP OR NO TIP?

Here are a few more situations of gratuity opportunities that we encounter on a regular basis—definitely times often overlooked when it comes to giving a gratuity.

Imagine this: The traffic is horrible and you arrive at home very late! It has been a very long day and there is nothing in the house for dinner; Ole' Mother Hubbard's cupboards are definitely bare. So you pick up the phone and order a pizza, or maybe you order a complete dinner from the French restaurant in town, and the delivery to your home has been confirmed to be exactly thirty minutes.

Now here is the question. Is this a gratuity-giving time? It sure is! This is a social gratuity time. Even though you are not seated at the pizza parlor or enjoying the candlelight dinner at Le Chateau restaurant downtown, using the flatware and china, and sipping on a glass of wine from a beautiful cut-crystal stem, service is being rendered by delivery to your home. You are not cooking the meal; it was late and your family is starving, and you called an eating establishment to prepare the meal and deliver the meal to your door. When your meal is delivered, the next step is to reach in your pocket and give a thank you in gratuity form, directly to the delivery person. Remember the standard base restaurant rule of ten percent of the order, less tax, is a good base or starting point for the suggested gratuity amount and is the proper thing to do.

Let's say it is the dead of winter in Aspen, Colorado. The temperature is below zero, and it is snowing. The roads are solid ice, and the drive to your home will be a tough one for any delivery service. Perhaps 15 percent as the starting base would be a nice thanks-a-bunch for driving through the winter storm and allowing you to stay warm and dry until dinner is served! Think about the cold and difficult drive, and quite possibly you, as the kind-hearted patron that you are, may reconsider the suggested base gratuity and bump the percentage up a bit. This is your choice, just like the anchovies on the pizza, and you are certainly welcome to give the delivery person a larger thank you tip, knowing that anything above suggested social percentage is always appreciated. Remember, the gratuity just may be the gas money for the delivery so try not to be too frugal on this decision. Yes, another one of those "did-you-know?" facts. Whether it be pizza or a restaurant meal delivered to your home, a gratuity for the delivery person is the proper thing to do and another example of a proper etiquette gratuity.

There are other types of deliveries that should be recognized with a thank you gratuity: a beautiful bouquet of flowers delivered by the corner florist or a special delivery package containing an item that you purchased on late night TV brought to your home by a delivery person. Offering a thank you gratuity for this delivery is a proper gratuity to be handed directly to the delivery person, of course, with a smile and the two words, thank you.

We have covered a lot of information on gratuity giving, so to help keep the information fresh in your minds, here is a brief summary of suggested gratuities for the services covered in the above paragraphs. This summary can be referred to each and every time you run into a wall, stimulating the questions in your brain: "When is it appropriate to give a gratuity or tip, and how much should it be?"

For some, it would be great to just follow a chart on these questions, always remembering that a social gratuity is an expected gratuity outlined by society and a proper gratuity can be determined by using good common sense. So, here you go—a list of social and proper etiquette suggested gratuities or tips.

SOCIAL AND PROPER ETIQUETTE SUGGESTED GRATUITIES OR TIPS

A monetary thank you for a job well-done

Occasion	Type of Gratuity	Suggested Amount
Market or grocery store	Proper gratuity	Two dollars and up. Make the offer; company policy may say no
At a restaurant	Social gratuity	15 percent and up (of the total before tax) in California, 10 percent and up (of the total before tax) in other states
Car wash	Proper gratuity	10 percent of the cost of service or 15 percent of the cost of service to be determined by the quality of service rendered.
Contracted home or office services	Social/ proper	Minimum of 50 percent of one month of service or determined by the level of service offered, the equivalent of one month of the service or a tangible gift at holiday time
Personal services	Social/ proper	10 percent plus (or more) of charge at the time
Home deliveries:	Proper gratuity	Three dollars as a base and the minimum of 10 percent and up of the purchased item amount

WHAT ABOUT PARKING VALETS?

When you drive into the valet circle of a hotel, resort, or club, what about that valet? Key word here is *valet*; now hold that thought! If there is a valet service available, and you choose to utilize the service by leaving your car with the valet to be parked and then pulled up to you when you are ready to depart the premises, you are socially expected to give the valet a gratuity. This can be tricky because there is often a fee to valet park as well. Keep the two fees separate in your mind and do not confuse the valet parking fee for the gratuity, as they are two different charges.

A charge for valet parking is usually the fee that will go toward the rental of the parking space, upkeep of that space, etc. The valet gratuity is above the valet fee; sometimes there may be a sign stating the amount. If not, beginning with a base of two dollars and working your way up is a good start. This gratuity is presented directly to the valet attendant as you are leaving the property, as a thank you for all of the courtesies that the valet attendant has offered to you—services such as opening the car door, parking the car, bringing the car back to you, and sometimes even offering you a cold bottle of water to enjoy on your travels. Again, this very nice service is acknowledged by offering a gratuity, a gratuity expected by society, along with a smile and, the two little words, thank you. Moving on.

The Door Person

Some may argue the subject of the door person, so let's visit this issue in detail, as it can be confusing.

You are a guest at a hotel or resort and you are planning on staying overnight. Each time you approach the doors of the hotel, the door person is there to open the doors for you, greeting you with a smile and a welcome. When you leave the hotel for a meal or some type of activity, the door person is there once again to assist you, offering a friendly welcome along with a smile.

Now, you are certainly not expected by society, nor prompted by proper etiquette to dip into your pocket each and every time you walk through the hotel doors. If that were the case, your pockets would be pretty puffy with rolled dollar bills. But it is suggested by social etiquette that at the end of your stay, a gratuity is offered to the door person for the kind and friendly services that have been rendered throughout your stay. This could be a five-dollar bill, given to the door person directly as a small token of appreciation, letting him know that his service was appreciated.

Possibly, you live in an apartment building, a flat, a complex, or even a suite in a hotel that you rent on a month-to-month basis, or was purchased as your home, and each and every morning when you leave for work and each and every evening when you return at the end of the day, the door person is there, opening the door and offering assistance in any way that may be needed. In this situation, it is suggested by both proper and social etiquette to acknowledge the continued service and recognize this faithful person with a thank you. The service offered by a door person could be considered as service from a contracted person and the same gratuity thank you gift is suggested. Of course, a gratuity would not be given every time the door is opened for you; however, you may wish to extend this thank you gratuity on a holiday or at the end of each month. The time is your choice; however, the offer of the gratuity is encouraged by society, and in this case, by proper etiquette as well. That same common sense recorder will click on in your brain, and with a handwritten thank you card or note with a nice monetary gift inside, your door person will accept your kind gift with sincere appreciation for the kindness offered by you; you both will feel great about the exchange.

CONTRACTED SERVICES—GRATUITY OR NO GRATUITY?

Now let's discuss vendors and service people who have been contracted for a special event—possibly a daughter's wedding or a corporate holiday party. The best approach to this situation is to begin by establishing a few social event terminology titles, or special event lingo. A gratuity at the end of the evening for contracted service people would be a social gratuity: an outlined, expected thing to do—a rule that is often forgotten by the host/hostess. The following pages on gratuity will address this gratuity issue in detail; so get ready to be inundated with many suggestions and social rules on this topic.

To make this simple, all contracted service people will be referred to as *vendors* and all people who would contract vendors will be referred to as *clients*. Whether your event is social, personal, corporate, or a Hollywood studio event, in order to ensure a successful event, vendors must be present! Based on the type of event you are hosting, the number of guests who will be attending, and the actual location of the event, you can be assured that there will be a list of vendors that must be contracted with to assure that your special day is a great success. All of these vendors will have their own special talents and perform their own special services or duties. Whether it is a wedding or a holiday party, held on an established site, such as a hotel, resort, country club, restaurant, or a site that will need to be transformed into a suitable event site, such as a private estate, open field, park, or abandoned building, to make the job a great success, contracted venders will be needed.

What is a vendor? Well, let's make this simple by providing a list of vendors that may be needed for the special day or the important event.

Caterer	Bartender	Wait staff	Pastry chef
Music	Floral décor	Plants/trees	Child care
Photographer	Videographer	Clergy/officiant	Stationer
Calligrapher	Banquet captain	Limousines	Valets
Sound systems	Entertainers	Planner	Lighting
Electrical	Visual effects	Hair stylists	Makeup artists

There are also numerous rentals that may be needed for your event, such as:

Tenting	Tables/chairs	Staging	Dance floors
Table dressings	Linens	Restrooms	Site kitchens
Air conditioning	Heating	Pool cover/decking	Subfloors
Dressing wagons			

If your event is planned on an off-site location, such as a private estate, an open field, a park, a ranch, a filming estate, or even an abandoned building, there are still additional vendors who will be needed, not to mention, insurance.

If you are having a wedding, mitzvah, baptism, or a religious or non-religious ceremony of any kind, outside the walls and restrictions of a church, temple, or synagogue, a person, male or female, should be contracted with who will preside over your ceremony. This person could be a priest, pastor, reverend, rabbi, cantor, or maybe even a close friend who has obtained a one-day deputyship from the county recorder offices in the area of the event in order to act as the officiant for the specific event, allowing him/her a legal right to perform a service. To simplify this group of very important vendors, the appropriate title would be officiant or clergy. Whatever the preferred title, this person is also considered a vendor.

If a location site is contracted, private or public, frequently a property, site, or banquet manager will be present at your event, acting as a representative or employee of the property owner; this person is also considered a vendor. It is less than safe to assume that a successful party just happens; it is planned and orchestrated to the very last detail. Therefore, it is always suggested that a client contract with an event producer or planner. A person who, for lack of a better choice of words, will act as the quarterback to oversee and assist with all setup and installation of all of the contracted rental items needed for the event, such as tenting, canopies, tables, chairs, lighting, electricity and generators, site kitchens, subflooring, air conditioning, heating, tabletop items, floral and plant installation, draping, and more; the list goes on. This person will be on-site to count in and confirm all of the items upon delivery, and repeat the count prior to pickup at the event's end to ensure that you, the client, are paying for exactly what you have ordered, nothing more or less, confirming that the order received is the order you placed. Let's be honest. You, as the client, are not going to take the time do this job, especially on that special day. That job is one of the many responsibilities of your planner. When all of the vendors arrive, such as the caterer and his or her staff, the musicians, the floral and space designers, the lighting crew, the valet service and limousine drivers, the photographers, and the videographers, the event producer or planner will be on-site to greet each of the vendors one by one, review their services, and communicate all of your wishes for the day. The event producer or planner will assist with the setup of the necessary equipment and supplies and even take care of the placement and supervision of the linens, chairs, and tabletop items. All of these jobs are done and overseen by your event producer or planner. Your event producer or planner is your quarterback, running back and forth with all of your dreams, wishes, and instructions for your special day to your vendors, leaving only one thing for you to worry about—you! What a wonderful relaxing and stress-free position to be able to experience. You will enjoy the event without worry because all of your dreams and wishes will be taken care of by your event producer or planner. It will be your perfect day, honored in your perfect way.

Each and every one of your vendors will be contracted with by you, the client, to render or perform a specific duty or talent. All vendors will be on-site at your event with one goal in mind: to work together as a team, ensuring that your special event will be the very best that it can be.

With that said, for a vendor, the gratuity is a social gratuity first, and a proper gratuity second. The following is a review of vendors that may be contracted for an event:

Caterer is a blanket term for the vendor who supplies the food and beverage for a special event. The banquet captain, bartenders, and the servers, whether the event is held at a hotel, resort, restaurant, country club, or on a contracted location site, would all fall under the category of caterers, and the social gratuity rule would apply to all. These people have been contracted on your behalf for your event. You may not have handpicked or interviewed each and every server; however, you can be assured that the catering establishment has done its job by reviewing the experience and fit of each worker on the job. Each member of the catering staff will attend to the needs of all of the guests attending your event by serving food and beverage. It is suggested, first by the social gratuity rule, and second by the proper etiquette rule, that a thank you gratuity is given to each member of the catering staff.

Time for a deep breath before continuing. Although the catering staff can be placed in the same category as service vendors at a restaurant, the gratuity rule is not the same. It would be financially impossible for the average person to give each member of the service staff the suggested restaurant 10 to 15 percent of the check and up. For a special event, a comfortable starting point for a gratuity to each member of the serving staff would be twenty dollars per person, which is most acceptable by society and proper etiquette alike. And both will give two thumbs up for honoring this etiquette rule. For the banquet captain, because this person is the supervisor of the entire staff and makes very sure that each and every guest is taken care of, a suggested base for an acceptable gratuity is a bit more. A starting base of fifty dollars and up shows that you, the host/hostess, are knowledgeable of the etiquette rule and appreciate the service rendered. These suggested amounts are a start; the actual amount is your decision. It is a thank you from you and your family, and it should be presented to the servers and banquet captain personally, if at all possible. At the end of the evening, when all is said and done, take a few moments to walk up to each and every catering vendor with your thank you gratuity in hand. It is a big task because at the end of a very long and exciting day, you and your family are still walking in the clouds and will most likely just want to return to your suite and relive the evening through conversation. If this is the case—we understand, as the vendors are most likely walking in the same clouds—there is a plan B. Plan B suggests that you have all of the gratuities placed in small envelopes, one for each vendor, which can be taken care of prior to the event. This will allow you time to think about what to say on the note that will be enclosed and to make a decision on how much each gift should be. Then, prior to the start of the festivities, hand the envelopes to your planner to distribute on your behalf. Plan A, doing it yourself, is the most desirable method to present the gratuity, however, Plan B is still warmly accepted. Either way, always remember that this little token is a thank you from you, the client, to the catering staff for a job well-done and should always be given from the heart, with a smile and a verbal thank you.

Along with the caterers, don't forget the bartenders; they are part of the serving staff as well, the people who keep the liquid refreshment flowing from beginning to end and who should be recognized as a very important part of the serving staff. The same suggested amount of gratuity is appropriate for the bartenders as is suggested for the other members of the catering team, with the exception of the banquet captain.

How about the pastry chef who will provide desserts and cakes? In a hotel, resort, restaurant, or country club, the pastry chef is a vendor who you may or may not have personal contact with. At many venues, the pastry chef is an in-house employee or is subcontracted by the establishment for this specialized service. And although you have the opportunity of deciding on style, flavor, and design of the cake or pastries, you may not have the option to actually sit down and meet one-on-one. If this is the case, offering the gratuity gift to the pastry chef is entirely up to you. There are no rules or guidelines directing or suggesting gratuity one way or the other in this situation. So my suggestion is to base your decision on the finished product.

How were the pastries?

Did the overall look take your breath away?

Was the flavor decadent, rich, and delightful?

If the answer is yes, even though you have no personal contact with the pastry chef, the gift is up to you. There are clients who contract with the pastry chef from an outside source, especially when hosting an event off-site. In this case, you do meet with the pastry chef, you do exchange ideas and suggestions, and you do taste the creations, which I highly recommend. So the question here is: do you offer a gratuity to the pastry chef? Referring to the social and proper etiquette rules, there is nothing that says you must; however, if the pastry chef's special creations for the cake or pasties are the most incredible ever, it is suggested that you say thank you by giving a gratuity or a small token of appreciation. Reach back into your memory bank to the file that says the right and proper thing to do and stimulate your common sense, and the rest is up to you.

A suggested amount for this vendor gratuity would be entirely up to you, but a good starting point would be 10 percent of the creation. If the finished cake is five hundred dollars, the thank you gratuity would be fifty dollars—a comfortable suggestion and an appreciated amount that says thank you for taking my breath away, the finished product created especially for me was amazing!

What about the music? There are a large number of people who feel that music is one of the most important elements in any event. A trio of strings, such as a violin, cello, and viola, a jazz trio consisting of a saxophone, a keyboard, and a bass violin, or even a solo harp or flute are all great examples of live music that can be contracted for a wedding ceremony, a cocktail reception, or even a celebration dinner party. For larger events, there are bands, which come in every shape and size and with talents in all styles of music. The number of the musicians, the sound level of their instruments, and the performance of the band should be determined by the number of guests at the event. The space in which the band is performing is also a big consideration when selecting that perfect band for the event. Live musicians, whether they are performing solo or in a group, are people who have taken years of lessons to perfect their trade and enhance their talent. Although it may seem like a lot of fun performing in the hot sun or on stage under bright lights, it really is hard work and for many musicians is their livelihood. There is no doubt that when we enjoy the talents of a musician or group, if the musicians do not also enjoy what they are doing, it will show in their performance. There is another old saying about music: music is the heart of a celebration. And when you think about it, it really is.

Looking at this gratuity issue in the same light as the catering staff, it probably would be less than realistic to come up with a perfect rule of thumb for an appropriate gratuity to give to each musician. Fifteen percent of the contract amount may be way out of your financial reach. But when you look back at your event and see all of your guests, including yourself, having the time of their lives, dancing and singing along with the music, you will realize that a gratuity is most appropriate for one of the main reasons your event was such a great success, the so-called heart of your celebration. A gratuity at the end of the evening is a socially expected thank you to be given to each band member or musician; however, the amount of the gratuity has no rules to govern it. If your band is contracted through a band agent, although the band may cost thousands, be assured that the band members do not receive the full amount charged. As an agent, there will be scheduling and organizing expenses, and a fee is charged for those services. The band members are usually paid a flat rate for a gig for a scheduled number of hours—usually one to two hours for the ceremony and the cocktail reception combined, and four hours for the dinner reception. After that, overtime is charged.

In the state of California, there is a musician union scale rate that is suggested and usually honored in payment of band members and other musicians by most reputable agencies. With this information in mind, I might suggest a good starting base of approximately fifty dollars per band member and anything greater than that amount is up to you. Once again, don't forget that smile and a big thank you as the gratuity is presented. And as the flames from the candle burn out on the guest tables, and the evening comes to an end, the smiles of appreciation that appear on the faces of the band members or musicians as they receive that thank you gratuity will again illuminate the room.

The following vendors—all contracted for a specific service for a special event and all having their own service contract, proposal, or invoice—are also vendors who put forth hours of work before and after the event to ensure that everything is perfect. Contracted vendors work together as a team to make sure that your perfect day is presented in your perfect way.

The florist is a vendor who may be contracted with to perform in many different capacities, such as all personal bouquets and *boutonnieres* for the bridal party, creating the unity area simply or with structured metals and florals, arranging floral pieces for the guest tables and other spaces in the room, or creating all of the floral designs in and around the site including the ceiling décor, and the draping, if requested. A florist may also contract for the placement of rental plants, trees, and foliage to enhance the décor of the room. And once again, there is no rule, socially or by proper etiquette, that says you must offer a gratuity. This personal decision would be based on the job rendered, and the amount of the gratuity would be determined by you. The actual preparation, including ordering of supplies, picking up the many flowers, and the preparing the florals, is done long before the actual event and is time-consuming, On the day of the event, the florist and the staff will begin at the crack of dawn, creating the many elements of floral design for any given event.

Does all of the hard work and creative energy put forth for an event require a thank you gratuity? I would certainly say yes. The services offered by a florist, no matter how small or large, will take many hours behind the scenes in purchasing, in preparation, and in creation, not to mention the delivery, setup, and takedown or strike, another vendor term. This is a perfect example of a proper etiquette gratuity, with no outlined rules or suggestions in print as to the amount of the gratuity, but definitely, a thank you in gratuity form is well-deserved for a florist.

The photographer, the video photographer, the lighting and electrical company, the sound producers, and the child care service are also vendors, contracted for a specific service for your special day. Upon entering a service contract with all of these vendors, the services and their performance should be outlined and the charge noted clearly on the contract. Do they require a gratuity? Photographers and video photographers all are providing a specific service that will surely enrich any special event, and there are no rules or guidelines, written or suggested, in any manuals as to whether or not a thank you gratuity is appropriate—so the decision is once again up to you. Each vendor makes a large contribution to the success of the event, and each vendor works as a team player to ensure that everything is perfect for the event.

What do you think? I think *yes* to all. A thank you gratuity is most assuredly in order, and yes, it is the proper thing to do.

All of the vendors reviewed above have extended a service, a job well-done on your behalf, and a proper etiquette gratuity would certainly be in order. Again, the amount of the gratuity is entirely up to you; possibly one hundred dollars is a good starting point, which would be far less than a minimum 10 percent suggested amount for other items. Review the event, assess the situation and the performance of each vendor, and then make your final decision. Any reasonable gratuity will be greatly appreciated—of course, given to the vendors personally at the end of the event, with a smile and a few words of thanks.

Here is a question. Would the vendor approach you if you did not offer the gratuity? Most certainly not, as event vendors are professionals who are most often ignored even though their part in the event is grand. The thank you gratuity given to these vendors is the energy that makes all of their hard work worthwhile.

A stationer and calligrapher are vendors who have established pricing for their products and services prior to the actual event. There is nothing that states that a monetary thank you is in order; however, even though there is no rule, the decision to extend a thank you gratuity in any shape or form is entirely up to you. Just remember that we all enjoy a thank you, and take the situation from there.

When an in-house or off-site valet service, a limousine, a shuttle, or any form of transportation service is contracted with, there is usually a gratuity already noted on the contract. A 10 to 15 percent gratuity is the going rate for this type of service vendor and is a fair starting point. And just like the add-on gratuity at a restaurant for a large group of guests, if you choose to bump that percentage up a bit, the decision is up to you. Should you decide that a larger gratuity is in order, another 5 percent above the noted add-on gratuity is a respectable increase—especially for exceptional service offered on your behalf, making the experience feel like sunshine at midnight for you and your guests.

The clergy or officiant and the event planner are usually the two vendors that are most personally involved with any client, and often the first two vendors to be overlooked when considering a thank you gift in gratuity form. The clergy or officiant, sometimes a friend or head of your place of worship, comes to the event on many levels—personally and guided by a higher power. There may be meetings or counseling sessions before and after the event date, and there is always the offer of availability to contact them at any time by placing a simple telephone call should there be any questions. The planner, in some cases, becomes a parent-like figure or a guidance counselor, sharing hours of information, suggestions, and ideas, and then following requests for the event to the letter, creating everything ever envisioned for the special day. Is it appropriate to offer a thank you in gratuity form to personal vendors? Again, there are no rules or guidelines that a gratuity is required, so perhaps this would be an ideal time to ask yourself a few questions. Did this personal vendor provide quality and personal service on your behalf? Was his or her time, knowledge, and service valuable and appreciated?

These are questions that can only be answered by you, the client; so after all is said and done, and you as the client are still walking in the clouds in complete satisfaction, the decision to offer a gratuity, a proper gratuity, is most appropriate—but again, the decision of the gift is entirely up to you.

For the clergy or officiant, the proper gratuity could be presented in the form of a donation to the church or temple, or to a charity that the church may be closely involved with. For the planner, a percentage of the total of the contract amount, something tangible or relaxing that you think would be special and appreciated, would be most appropriate and welcomed.

This is a very difficult one for me. From a professional standpoint, I feel odd making suggestions with regard to a gratuity to the event planner. However, looking back on all of the amazing clients that I have had the honor to assist over the years, and reliving the many wonderful thank you gratuities and gifts I have received, I can honestly say that whatever is decided on, will be blissfully received and deeply appreciated. Please be sure that the thank you comes from your heart and is presented personally by you, given with a smile, together with a few words of thanks. Remember, a thank you in gratuity or gift form is never expected by either of the two personal vendors just covered, but always deeply appreciated.

Last, but not least, in the list of important vendors are the rental companies. These companies provide the use of tenting and canopies, tables, chairs, and table dressings, such as china, flatware, and stemware or glassware. They provide staging and dance floors and linens and carpets. For off-site locations, rental companies provide restrooms, standard and VIP, and site kitchens, such as the ovens and stovetops that are used to cook the food, including coffee percolators and servers that perk and then fill the cups at the end of the meal—all of these are rental vendors. There are also the special item rental companies, companies that will cover a swimming pool with a bridge, dance floor, or dining surface, create a carpeted ballroom on top of a football field or tennis court, project a night sky on the top of a tent, heat a space on a cold winter's night, or cool a space on a warm summer's evening.

As for gratuity, rental vendors are vendors. A contract or invoice is created, listing in detail each item that has been rented for an event. A delivery and pickup charge is included on the contract, and in some cases a damage surcharge will be added as insurance for the rental company that the rental items that go out to an event will be returned in good condition. What you will not see on a rental invoice is a gratuity added to the invoice, opening the door to the question of whether or not a rental company deserves a gratuity.

Probably not the rental company itself—there is a profit margin built into the rental charges. There will probably be a charge for the delivery and pickup of said items, and the surcharge, insurance, replacement, and damage or lost charges may be included in the invoice. But a thank you gift for the delivery people, who are actually putting the sweat and backbone into the installation of the event, and will only be receiving a flat hourly rate, would be greatly appreciated. So, yes, it would be a very nice gesture to give the delivery people a thank you gratuity for a hard job offered on your behalf. The delivery people are the worker-bee vendors who load the rental items on the delivery trucks, drive the rental items to the event site, unload the rental items from the trucks, and then place the rental items in the areas as instructed by the contract. At the end of the evening or the next day, based on the terms of the contract, the delivery people will return to the event site for the pickup of the rental items. When the truck is loaded, they drive back to the rental warehouse or company, unload the rental items from the delivery trucks, and punch out for that job. Delivery people have the hardest job of all: loading, lifting, and arranging, all in a specific time frame. It is a job that certainly would not be done by the client. So when it comes to a thank you gratuity, you make the call. Reach back into your memory bank, wake up that file on common sense and proper etiquette, and then give this situation a few minutes of thought. I can comfortably say that the proper gratuity rule would certainly come into play in this case, and a thank you would be in order. Any reasonable monetary gratuity would be appreciated, and a suggested base would be five, ten, or twenty dollars per delivery person. It is your call if you should choose to increase the amount. As you think about the many trucks filled with the rental items that were needed to complete the event service, the amount of the thank you gift of gratuity to the delivery people may increase. A moment's thought of common sense or proper etiquette may be used as the guideline, but the bottom line is that the final decision is up to you.

The subject of gratuity and tips is probably larger than one would expect. The reason that it is a very important subject—and one that is ignored on many occasions—is because there are so many theories and stories circulating about what is proper and what is not. Now you have the facts on this subject, simply stated, and you are able to take the information and apply it to your everyday life. Suggestions outlined by society, guidelines directed by proper etiquette, good old common sense motivated by the lessons you have learned—and the rest is up to you.

The importance of social and proper etiquette regarding gift giving, gratuity, and tips leaves most of us with questions. Not anymore! Here is a scenario that I am certain you will now have the answer to.

Let's give it a try:

You and your family are finally taking a well-deserved vacation. You will be out of town for the weekend and your dog, Murphy, will be staying home. You will only be gone for a couple of days so there is no need to stop the mail or newspaper delivery; your next door neighbor has kindly offered to watch over Murphy, bring in the newspaper and mail, and keep watch of your home. When you get home from your weekend vacation, what do you do?

A. Run into the backyard to check on Murphy then yell, "thanks" over the fence!

B. Walk over to the neighbor's house, knock on the door with a heartfelt thank you gift in hand and a personal note attached, and thank them for watching over things in your absence.

C. Call your neighbor on the phone and let them know that you have returned and all is well.

Correct answer is B: You PERSONALLY walk over to the neighbor's house, knock on the door with a heartfelt thank you gift in hand and a personal note attached, and thank them for watching over things in your absence. They were kind enough to perform the duty of dog sitter, newspaper and mail pickup service, and neighborhood watch agent while you were away, and this definitely says, that by proper etiquette, a neighborly thank you gift is in order.

Chapter Nine

Invitations and Announcements

THERE IS A social statement used when referring to stationery: "An invitation is the introduction to one's entire event."

At this time, I ask that you file this intriguing first sentence of this chapter into your memory bank, as it is certain that you will be asked to reach back and pull out the meaning of that statement and apply it throughout the pages ahead.

Basically, we all know what an invitation or announcement is, and we have all received examples of both, beginning when we were children and continuing throughout our elementary and secondary school years, and well into our adult and professional lives. Over the years, we all have sent out invitations and announcements to friends, family, and professional associates, both formally and informally, and a few of these mailings may even have been homemade. For those who are in high school and even in college, or parents of children in that age group, an introduction to the flyer-type invitation has most likely been received. It is a very informal form of an invitation to a party or get together—a blanket invitation or announcement, often brightly colored, on letter-weight paper with bold print and "no reply necessary" printed on the bottom. This blanket flyer has probably been hiding in the mailbox or in a stack of books in a teen's room. All of the needed information has been included, and there may also be some interesting artwork splashed over the entire page. The paper selected may be a color that will never be seen again. As for presentation, *very, very, informal* would probably be the best description.

Although the blanket method is probably not the most proper example of an invitation or announcement, surprisingly, it does serve the same purpose as a properly worded or traditional invitation or announcement, in a more cost-effective, creative manner, but certainly in a less sophisticated way.

Revisiting our friend, *Webster's Dictionary,* the word *invitation* means: an act of inviting, a message used in inviting, or an enticement, simply stating that an invitation is the introduction to any planned event, inviting guests to a social gathering to include all of the needed event information for the celebration.

The word *enticement,* also used in the definition of the word *invitation* offered by Mr. Webster, lends a somewhat mysterious tone. In short, an invitation can also be a form of enticement, meaning to attract by offering pleasure, enjoyment, or reward. Hence, the act of inviting and the measure of attraction suggested in Mr. Webster's printed and accepted definition of an invitation is both inviting and enticing.

Looking back on the many invitations that have been received over the years, there have probably been some that have brought a smile to your face, a few that have possibly raised an eyebrow, and perhaps several that have left you scratching your head in complete amazement. There were perhaps one or two that even stimulated the curiosity of origin, prompting the question, "What were they thinking when *that* invitation was selected?" When any reaction other than a calm, very nice invitation is experienced, it is time to go back to the basics and simply remind yourself that the invitation is the proper written form of inviting, stating all of the necessary information required for an upcoming event that is scheduled to take place sometime soon. And that will be that!

An announcement is also a form of information regarding an event; however, the information included on an announcement is announcing an event that has already taken place. An announcement is always mailed by the announcer after the fact. In order to fully understand what an announcement is, we need to revisit the meaning of the word *announce.*

To announce is to bring information to the attention of the public, the family, friends, or even business associates. To announce also means giving news of the arrival of a person, place, event, or subject that has already happened or taken place.

Once again, by doing a little homework and looking up the meaning of the word *announcement* in a dictionary, it simply defines it as the act of announcing, a proclamation.

In this chapter, we will review the highlights of both invitations and announcements. We will touch on the basics of proper wording and various presentations of both. We will outline appropriate occasions when an invitation or announcement might be sent, and we will also take a sneak peek into the world of style and designs that are readily available to us all, and of course, we cannot forget the importance of basic etiquette in which all of this information should be applied.

This chapter will also serve as a simple guide as to when it is appropriate to extend a very casual invitation or announcement by just picking up the telephone or sending out an e-mail to invite someone or to announce an event. Are you ready to begin? Here we go.

An invitation is extended to family, friends, and professional associates for an upcoming event, such as a birthday, a shower in celebration of an upcoming birth or wedding, a graduation from high school or university, or a holiday gathering or dinner. An invitation is also extended to request the attendance at an awards dinner or ceremony, company function, and even a party selling housewares, jewelry, candles, or other items. No matter how large or small the gathering may be, or what type of an event is being planned, when one receives an invitation, it is always proper to reply. Either yes, you will be attending, or no, you are not able to attend. No lengthy explanation is required as to why you will or will not be in attendance; a simple yes or no will suffice. If the invitation is to a formal event, the reply would be in writing, and most often a reply/response card will be included in the invitation. If the occasion is a more casual event and there is no reply card enclosed, it is socially acceptable to reply either by placing a telephone call and speaking to the host or hostess directly, by writing a personal note and sending it to the host or by making a personal visit to the person hosting the event. In the world of computers and the ease and efficiency of e-mails, a properly written e-mail is acceptable if this is the usual manner of communication with the busy host/hostess—however it is not socially proper. It is always suggested that a reply in any situation is done by writing a personal reply note. The note will only take a minute to write and presents itself in a very caring manner; proper and personal is the suggested road to take.

An announcement can also be extended to family, to friends, and to professional associates when announcing or proclaiming a special event that has already taken place. A marriage, the birth of a child, a graduation from school, or a promotion are all occasions when an announcement is extended and, of course, always mailed following the event date.

And as long as we are on the subject, this is the perfect opportunity to mention that there are exceptions to the mailing rule of an announcement: when you are announcing the opening of a business, and when you are being transferred or moving out of the area, but are continuing your profession.

These forms of announcements definitely fall under the definition of proclaiming the information, and in these two noted situations, can be proclaimed prior to the actual start date or first day of business in a new area.

An announcement will not be confused with an invitation because the mailing is not announcing a party; it is simply a proclamation or announcement to the public, to family, and to friends, that the doors of your new business or the address of the new location of your business will be open on a specific date.

Even in these two situations, in actuality, it still is an announcement; therefore, making the trip to the post office after the move is the socially suggested action to take.

With the announcement, there follows an acknowledgment. Acknowledging the announcement is usually done by sending a card or a gift, or making a personal visit to the honored guest. An announcement, unlike an invitation, is not an invite to the announced event, so there will be no need for schedule rearranging. Please do not plan on showing up, as the event has already taken place. However, like an invitation to a party or celebration, sending a gift is appropriate and always the proper thing to do. An announcement is a social courtesy of notification of an event that has already taken place, and the next step to the announcement is an acknowledgment of the event in the form of a gift, a card, or a letter; the choice of the acknowledgment is up to you.

Although it seems that many of the etiquette rules honored years ago, displaying formality and proper etiquette, are now somewhat things of the past, in the world of invitations and announcements, one still must remember that an invitation, announcement, or any form of informational mailing, is and will always be, the introduction to the entire event yet to come or one that has already taken place. Proper format, wording, and style of the invitation, announcement, or mailing will always set the stage for the occasion. Traditionally, this statement simply says that you, as the inviter or host/hostess of the event, has put forth the love, time, and care in the preparations of the event—as well as an expression of good manners and social grace. By sending an invitation with kissing frogs with brightly colored ink, or a blanket flyer with unidentifiable artwork, the mailing seems to say "come as you are and see what happens." The statement you make on your invitation or announcement is in your hands.

It is time to go back to the first sentence of this chapter. You remember; the *intriguing* sentence?

Let's begin with an invitation. An invitation can be purchased from a card store, ordered from a stationer, or personally created. If the event is a fun, casual event, the invitation can be created keeping that thought in mind. A child's birthday party, a sweet sixteen party, a barbeque, or a Super Bowl party can all be introduced on an invitation, self-made and created by the host/hostess, in an array of styles and decorative trims. An invitation for a casual event does not have to be stuffy or formal—quite the contrary. The invitation can be whatever is desired as long as a few simple steps are followed, making the invitation proper. For that matter, a formal invitation does not have to be intimidating or over the top. It just has to be correct, and directed by social and proper etiquette rules.

There are a few steps that should always be followed when selecting an invitation, formal or casual. Three important steps must be present, which I call the *Simple Three—A, B, C.*

A. Ask, or invite to an event

B. Body, or information of the event

C. Conclusion, or closing to the invitation

The options are unlimited, opening the doors to so many styles, designs, colors, and forms; however, the top priority before making that final decision should always be the *Simple Three—A, B, C.*

A. Ask

B. Body

C. Conclusion

Beginning with the selection of a casual invitation for a birthday, holiday gathering, or backyard barbeque, just remember, this is a casual function, so let the creative juices flow. Make it fun, make it colorful—include dimensions and add texture and attachments. The door is open to include a kiss of whimsical sparkly by using a bit of "*bling*," such as crystals, beading, or foils, always incorporating the theme to the event and giving the invited guests a sneak peek into the adventures that lay ahead. Feathers are fun and can be used in the invitation and carried throughout the entire event. When used tastefully, they can be an added surprise to the entire package.

If the event is a formal event, the invitation should be created with that in mind. No kissing creatures, or pop-out figures, and no metallic colors. Use basic colors of ink; some colored ink is acceptable, but generally should be kept for a more casual event. Look back a few years into the social old world etiquette suggestions of ivory or white card stock. The paper weight must always be heavy enough to stand up proudly when holding the card upright from a bottom corner using the support of only a thumb and a forefinger. If the paper weight is not at least the weight of a nice card stock, the invitation will bend like the branches of a weeping tree, and the statement it will send will be less than impressive! This visual always reminds me of the trash bag commercial: "Hefty, hefty, hefty! Wimpy, wimpy, wimpy."

Can you see it? I just love how perfect this commercial jingle paints the picture of a wimpy-weight card stock. The card stock that should be used on an invitation should never be less than eighty-to-one-hundred-pound weight.

That way, the invitation will stand proudly, whether it be for a backyard barbeque or a ballroom event at the Ritz.

When in doubt of a selection or creation of the perfect invitation to any occasion, formal or casual, the traditional basics of a proper invitation is the safe path to follow, once again using proper wording and my rule of the *Simple Three—A, B, C.*

A basic tuxedo, or federal-style card, and the formal, yet standard, inks of black or charcoal embossed, engraved, or letter-pressed on a nice ivory or white card stock are once again the safe direction to follow when creating a formal invitation. All are elegant selections and all make the statement that the entire creation of the mailing is proper, correct, and formal. This ultimate exercise of formality in presentation of an invitation will advise a guest of the elegance that lies ahead.

As said many times in the past, common sense really is a driving force of simple grace, social and proper etiquette. Remember that every invitation that is sent out by any host or hostess should be a representation of that individual, of their personality, and of the upcoming event. We are not all made from a single mold, or created in the same cookie-cutter fashion, and neither should anything that is created and sent out by us be done in that manner. Be creative and apply proper etiquette when selecting the perfect invitation for the perfect event. Simple grace, social and proper etiquette, will never go out of style or remotely imply that the mailing was done in an uncaring manner, even if the event is a casual event. Simple grace, and social and proper etiquette, in the application of an invitation are the tools that are directed by common sense and etiquette and are completely owned by the host or hostess, or creator of the invitation. Apply the tools correctly, properly, and with good taste, and the selection that you have made will belong to you.

There will never be a time when the age of a person can, or should be used as an excuse in the selection of an improper mailing. Nor is there an age limit on hosting a party, or planning a gathering to share in good times. The resources to fund the event may come from an outside source, but the inviter will remain the host/hostess, and nothing can change that fact. Proper is proper, for young and old alike. With that in mind, there can never be an excuse for a party or event introduced with a stationery *faux pas*, which, as we all know, in French means "not real" or in the world today terms, "big mistake!" When thinking about an invitation, do some homework and let common sense, simple grace, and social and proper etiquette be your guides. The path these tools will lead you along will always be the correct path in selecting the perfect invitation for the perfect celebration.

As a parent or guardian planning a party for a child's birthday or presentation of an award, the invitation should follow the same *Simple*

Three—A, B, C rule. For a religious recognition, apply the same steps; however, be aware of the church or temple guidelines that must be followed. Make a phone call or visit and check with the person who will be in charge of the religious portion of the celebration to confirm that the invitation selected is in order and following the religious guidelines applicable to the function.

A birthday party can be more casual and fun; a nice start in finding the perfect invitation would be to select a theme for the party, and again follow the *Simple Three—A, B, C* steps. By selecting a theme to the event, and incorporating that theme into the creation of the invitation, the decorations, the cake, the entertainment, and even the favors of the party, the theme will assist in making every detail of the event fall into place perfectly. Make all decisions meaningful and fun and incorporate colorful ideas—all of which will lend a helping hand in personalizing the event for all of the guests, and especially for a special honored guest. When the finished invitation is received by guests, the personality of the honored guest will shout loud, properly, and with clarity, allowing the guests to open the door to a wonderful event.

LIONS AND TIGERS AND BEARS, OH MY!

Your event is a special day and it should be presented in a very special way. For a child's birthday, involving the child in the actual making of the invitation can be a lot of fun and makes the experience a personal expression for the children and not a boring or cookie-cutter, "I-really-don't-care" invitation to a party. Follow the same *Simple Three—A, B, C* steps that would be followed when creating any invitation. As you begin your own personal masterpiece, don't forget the paste for the cutouts, or the glue gun for the crystals. Any small tangible items that can be attached to your invitation can give the creation the dimensions that are needed to pop rather than sink. And all of the creative ideals and expressions of the honored guest's personality will be remembered as this invitation, an invitation created from the heart especially for the guests who are invited, will be received with excitement and anticipation, resulting in a very nice compliment to you.

When do you send an invitation? An invitation should be mailed through the postal service for all gatherings with over ten guests. Believe it or not, social etiquette does suggest, more than ten, pull out the pen.

Whether the invitation or announcement is purchased from a card store, printed by a stationer, or created in the family kitchen with loving hands, a postal mailing received will be appreciated and a mailing in passing, will most often be forgotten. We all know what a postal mailing is, but what is a mailing in passing? Good question and I just happen to have the answer. A mailing in passing is a verbal invitation, perhaps extended over the fence to a neighbor, or to a friend while standing in line at the market waiting for checkout. A mailing in passing, although printed, can be an e-mail. Personally, the receiver of a mailing in passing oftentimes may feel that the invitation was extended as an afterthought. A tangible invitation received through the mail is a sign of importance; not only for the upcoming event, but to the invited guest as well. The host/hostess has taken the time to create, stamp, and drop in the mail an invitation to a celebration to an important person: the guest that will receive the invitation. Pretty special, don't you agree?

This bit of wisdom goes back to my business training and it really does make a lot of sense—common sense. As professionals, it is safe to state that in the business world, one statement that holds true is that one is expected to remember everything that is heard and everything one is told.

Realistically, this statement is probably the most ridiculous statement that has ever passed through the lips of any employer. Although there are many brilliant people in the world who have the amazing gift of a photographic memory, to remember everything is really stretching it and is more than can be expected from a genius robot, let alone a human. So, the suggested safety net is to write it down. If whatever you hear and whatever you are told is written down, it is not easily disputed, nor is it easily forgotten. When it is written down, all of the details and the information are readily available to you by reading the print. When one receives a written, or printed invitation or announcement, there is a visible commitment to a function. And with this commitment, a reply must be made in a timely manner—in writing.

When information is received in print form, it is written down in the guest's planner or on a calendar in plain sight, locking in the date and confirming that if anything else does come up, the written date is already committed! When the information is not written down, it is not fact, and therefore, not a commitment, nor can the subject matter be backed up by any notes, dates, or comments, so when the calendar is scanned, the date is open—brain freeze—forgotten.

Posting a notice to a function in the company meeting room or school lunch room is not the proper way of inviting anyone to any upcoming function or event. This form of invitation or announcement may work as a group reminder, or a notice of instructions, or disciplinary action, such as, "please remember to turn off the lights," or "no pets in the lunch room," but should never be used as a form of invitation or announcement to any social or corporate event.

Can you imagine entering the foyer of a ballroom, and on the massive ornate double-oak-carved entrance doors leading into the elegant ballroom ahead, you see a paper sign, posted on the doors with a couple of strips of scotch tape holding the sign in place that reads, "Presidential Ball, come on in!"

Oh my gosh, I don't think so! An invitation would be mailed out a minimum of six weeks and a maximum of eight weeks prior to the event date in a formal format, following the *Simple Three—A, B, C* rules, and a reply card would be mailed back to the host/hostess, with a proper reply to the invitation no less than three weeks and the minimum of two weeks prior to the event date. And upon entering the grand and elegant foyer leading up to the massive ornate double-oak-carved entrance doors into the Presidential Ballroom, it is more likely that you would see a proper and correct information board, presented in a gold leaf or brass-framed, easel-style stand, directing you to the proper function space that would read: "Presidential Ball."

You would not see signs created in computer print, or hand-scribbled on colored paper with pieces of scotch tape barbarically taped to an existing post, announcing the event that lies ahead. Remember, the social stationery statement says an invitation is the introduction to the entire event.

True statement. A formal invitation to an event requires a mailing date of a minimum of six weeks and a maximum of eight weeks from the event date, especially if a meal is involved. Look at a calendar, beginning with the event date and count backward, eight weeks from the scheduled event date. That date is the date the host/hostess of the event will be standing in the post office, mailing the invitations, which will hopefully also be hand-cancelled. To have an invitation hand-cancelled at the post office rather then sent through the meter not only protects the thicker envelope, but is visually more acceptable. There will be no damage to the envelope, not even a little munch, and no big, bold ticker number across the guest name. It takes a few moments longer and, oftentimes, you may have to hand-cancel the envelopes yourself, but the end result is worth every moment that it takes, and all the red ink that is left behind on your hands. All you have to do is ask the postmaster and chances are more likely than not, the answer will be yes.

The date on the reply card for a formal event, such as a wedding, according to the rules of proper etiquette, is suggested three weeks prior to the event. Beginning with the event date and counting backward a total of three weeks, is the date that would be printed on the reply card, requesting that all of the replies should be returned to the client or host/hostess of the event. A lovely self-addressed, stamped envelope in the same card stock and style as the invitations will hold the reply card and will, of course, be properly enclosed in the mailing of the invitation. The reply card itself will be returned to the client bearing the name(s) of the invited guest and an *"accepts with pleasure"* or *"declines with regret,"* carefully checked in the appropriate space provided. If the guest receiving the invitation and reply card is a residence of the United States, the reply envelope will be stamped with the appropriate postage stamp, preferably matching the stamp(s) on the mailing envelope of the invitation.

NEVER should an invitation or reply envelope bare a postage meter stamp, even though Daddy has a postage meter at the office.

Hark, I feel questions in the air, good questions, which apply to weddings, to baby or wedding showers, and to corporate and social gatherings. Are the invitations mailed out two months prior to the actual event date? And why is the requested reply date three weeks prior to the event date? Thank you for asking; I just happen to have the answers directed, of course, by social and proper etiquette rules, outlined years ago, which are used as a guide to those questions in the world today.

For the mailing of the invitation, a minimum of six weeks and a socially suggested maximum of eight weeks are suggested as the mailing date in consideration of the guests invited to the event, the facility where the event will be held, and the catering department. For the guests, this time frame allows ample time to make the necessary arrangements in order to attend the event.

In this time frame, if the guests are traveling from another state or country, there will be ample time to make the needed reservations for overnight accommodations in the area of the event location, or in the surrounding areas of the event location. This time frame also allows ample time for the guests to reserve travel arrangements, whether they be by car, air, train, or sea and even to obtain a passport if need be.

And finally, it is the perfect amount of time to keep the invitation to an event fresh in the minds of the guests and also allow for any revisions to a schedule, if necessary.

Mailing an invitation prior to the eight-week date can encourage two situations that, as a host/hostess, it must be agreed are neither complimentary nor considerate.

First: The receipt of an invitation more than two months from the event date is a very long time to keep the information fresh in one's mind. The invitation could be misplaced, and on occasion, a second important obligation could pop up, and if the guest is not looking at a calendar, may just accidentally double-book that date. But most importantly, when one receives an invitation to a formal event, especially to a wedding or a landmark birthday celebration, for example, three months prior to the event date, it is a social and silent flag that might imply the number one invitation *faux pas*—the B guest list. The B guest list as a consideration to a guest list for even a ten-guest casual event, is completely improper and should be a book on its own—a second pot of names, if you will, to be added to the original guest list if guests from that list A decline the invitation. There are no rules and no guidelines that a B guest list is not acceptable; just common sense and human consideration that if whomever is invited from the B guest list were aware of the fact that the invitation extended to them was a second choice because the host's/hostess's first choice could not attend, an acceptance may be with reservation. Personally, I would not be complimented to receive an invitation to a special event as a second thought, would you?

Second: A formal invitation also implies a planned meal, such as a dinner, mandating caterers and serving staff. Again, common sense implies that in order to be prepared for a meal that must be served to a group of guests, special guests, perfectly and professionally, certain duties must be taken care of by the catering staff prior to the big day.

Beginning with the mailing date of your invitation, even in the busiest of times, the guests will begin to return their reply cards, confirming that they will or will not be attending the event.

The "three weeks from the event date" requested on the reply card will give the host/hostess a grace period approved by proper etiquette to finalize the guest count before it is required by the caterer.

The host/hostess or client can begin to contact the guests who have delayed the return of their replies, taking the countdown to the two-week mark, the date required and requested by most contracts with the caterer to turn in the final count; a guest count that the host/hostess will be obligated to pay on. The two-week mark, or two weeks prior to the event date, allows the caterer time to order food and supplies, contract with the perfect serving staff, and create any of the items of special order that will assist in making the special event a dream come true. It is a courtesy to the catering staff as well as to the location that has been contracted for this event and also moves the host/hostess or client one step closer to the end of the details of the orchestration of the event.

When all of the guests have replied, the guest count for food, beverage, and the rentals and contracts for all of the vendors involved in the event have been advised, the host/hostess can begin the placement of the guests at the guest tables—another step toward the magic and excitement of a special event that will be remembered for a lifetime.

Please forgive the event planner approach to this explanation, however, one must admit, now there is absolutely no question on the subject of an invitation and the purpose of the three weeks prior to the event date reply card. It offers consideration of the guest, courtesy to the host/hostess, and creating of the final seating chart. Agreed?

An announcement may also be purchased from a card store, custom-ordered from a stationer, or personally made. Like an invitation, the *Simple Three—A, B, C* rule should be followed with one small difference. *A* is for *announcement*, rather than asking, or introducing the event in the first part of your mailing, the host/hostess will be announcing; or proclaiming an event that has already taken place.

A: Announcement

B: Body

C: Closing

The purpose of mailing an announcement is to proclaim or announce an event that has already taken place, A is for Announcement. These same basic *Simple Three—A, B, C* steps should be followed when applying pen to paper for your announcement—and for that matter, just about everything and will guide you down the proper and correct path to the perfect announcement, or proclamation of a very important event that has already taken place.

A: Announcement

B: Body

C: Closing

Sending an announcement is a common method of announcing the birth or adoption of a baby or child. It is also a common mailing when announcing the graduation of a student, or the new address of a residence after a move. Like an invitation, this mailing can be sent to family, to friends, and also to business associates—even to friends of friends and acquaintances from long ago. All of the wonderful and creative ideas one may have in the creation of an announcement can be the expressions of who you are, what you are announcing, and where you are going, and should be included in your mailing. By the same token, all of the rules, guidelines, and suggestions on proper and social etiquette, proper wording, and presentation should also be incorporated into the announcement. As you begin the approach in the creation of the perfect announcement, just like the approach taken in the creation of the perfect invitation, a large door will open to many papers, styles, and options of printing to choose from. Just remember that the direction that should be taken is the road to simple grace and common sense, and when used as your guide, will ensure that your announcement will be perfect.

WHEN TO SEND AN ANNOUNCEMENT

An announcement is to announce or proclaim an event that has already taken place, a notice to friends, family, business associates, and other acquaintances that an event, special and important, has taken place in your life, and you wish to share the amazing event with others.

There is no reply requested or required when sending an announcement because there is no event to attend. There is no outlined time frame as to when the announcement is mailed, with the followings exceptions and a few suggestions:

THE ARRIVAL OF A BABY OR CHILD INTO YOUR HOME

The social suggestion for the mailing of this type of an announcement is within three months of the arrival date. Waiting longer than three months may imply that the steam behind the mailing is gift motivated. An announcement is a proper method of announcing a birth or an adoption of a new member of your family. It is a very exciting time for everyone and it is proper, as well as fun, to share the exciting news with friends, family, and business associates.

A MARRIAGE

The social and proper etiquette rule states that for the announcement of a marriage, the mailing should be the week following the actual event date—I always suggest that the mailing be done the first working day following the event if at all possible. Never send an announcement prior to the wedding date as the mailing may be mistaken as an invitation. An announcement for a marriage is a courtesy notice to people who could not attend the event due to distance, to health or age, or because they really do not know the bridal couple well enough to be invited to the event, but are friends or business associates of the parents or family of the couple.

GRADUATION FROM HIGH SCHOOL, UNIVERSITY, OR A TECHNOLOGY CENTER

It is socially suggested that the announcement be mailed the week following the actual date of the event, however, a great number of the graduation announcements have been sent out over the past ten years that are actually invitations to the graduation ceremony and not an announcement at all. Does this mailing fall under social and proper etiquette, or did the printer make a big mistake? Because this type of mailing is called an announcement, but is also used as an invitation, it is difficult to place it in a category at all. Unless you are close to the graduate, when this mailing is received, it is safe to say that it has been sent to announce the graduation of the individual and not as an invitation to the ceremony. Because of the limited space at an actual graduation ceremony, an invitation would only be extended to a limited few, so on this one, when in doubt, ask!

Retirement or Promotion

Should you choose to announce a retirement or promotion, social and proper etiquette would suggest that the announcement be mailed the week following the actual date of the event. The announcement would serve as a notice of the retirement or promotion of a person. If there is a celebration honoring the person on this achievement, and there will be a celebration, an invitation should always be mailed to those guests on the list.

New address or a location move

We all have friends and family who come into our lives and then move away. A new address or location move announcement is a method of notifying all of the friends, family, and even business associates of the move and supplying everyone with the new contact information. The announcement actually does not have guidelines or suggestions offered by society or proper etiquette as to the suggested mailing date. This type of an announcement is a courtesy for friends, family, business associates, and acquaintances and one of convenience for the party who has moved, and should be mailed after the location move, and when the actual and correct address of the new home or business has been occupied. This type of an announcement would be a mailing or notification of information in written form, again proper and correct, and, without question, would follow all of the steps outlined in the *Simple Three—A, B, C*; created and then mailed to the appropriate people on the list.

When the mailing list has been created and the announcement is in hand, properly addressed and stamped, the announcements will be mailed out. Please, no clear labels generated on the computer. Just like mailing an invitation, all announcements are mailed out at the same time. If the announcement is the notification of the new address and contact information following a location move, the announcements will be mailed when, and only when, the new location is being occupied. Mail sitting in a mailbox with no residents living inside is an invitation to Harold Home Invader, remember? As stated earlier, some people feel that sending out an announcement for a business prior to the actual move is acceptable. Social and proper etiquette would suggest that it would be more appropriate to wait until the move has been made, then mail the announcements. And keep in mind, the same Harold can invade home OR business.

Invitations and announcements, special ordered, custom designed, or made by hand, are all very important mailings in our society. Blended with love and combined with an array of ingredients including social and proper etiquette, then finished with a dash of common sense, then sprinkled with a kiss of simple grace, makes for an amazing recipe for a successful event.

Chapter Ten

Stationery

AN ENTIRE BOOK could be written on the subject of stationery, but for now, you are all invited to take a trip down the beautiful road lined with all the colors of the rainbow, and to explore several important items that can probably be identified by sight, but perhaps are not completely understood as to how they are used. The items in question are the many pieces of stationery and their use is, of course, proper. This journey has already been briefly visited in the chapter on invitations and announcements, as both are commonly used forms of stationery—however there are more, many more uses of stationery. So sit back and enjoy as we travel down this long and incredible road of stationery, the many items available, and the proper use of each one.

Once again, returning to our friend, Mr. Webster, and his dictionary, we are looking up the definition of the word *stationery*, which reads, "writing materials, especially paper and envelopes."

Writing materials, such as paper, note cards, single-sided cards, journals or ledgers, and even diaries are all items that can be listed under the category of stationery. In simple terms, most any form of writing material can be placed, properly and respectfully, under stationery. And envelopes and the source of mailing, containing, or presenting these items, are also considered writing materials or stationery.

A THANK YOU

The journey on stationery begins with the most commonly used stationery: invitations and announcements. Continuing along the road are a few additional, and very important items of stationery which are a thank you note, a thank you card, or a thank you letter. This form of stationery should be as familiar to us all as the invitation and announcement. Upon receiving an invitation or announcement, a gift usually follows, so a thank you note can be viewed as a couple to, or partner of, the invitation or announcement, so to speak; but, unfortunately, is often forgotten.

Remember the holiday gift that you spent days thinking about and saving for? And when you had all of the hard-earned pennies together, you shopped until you dropped, then finally found the perfect gift for your special friend. The gift was wrapped with love and care, not forgetting any of the personal touches, and when presenting this labor of love to your friend, the papers were torn from the package and sailed down to the floor, displaying the gift in open sight for all to see. Then in a split second, it was all over, and your friend was on to the next package. No words of thanks, no "great gift," nothing!

Alright, perhaps this type of reaction from the receiver of the gift is somewhat understandable. It was a celebration, there were stacks of other gifts to be opened, and the air was filled with the energy of excited people, all ready to present more gifts. But then, following the celebration, days and weeks passed by and nothing; not a thank you note, no thank you letter or card, not even an e-mail or follow-up phone call letting you know that all of the time and effort that was put into the gift was appreciated or even credited to the right giver.

Now, before the emotion takes over this situation, let's back up and review things one more time. Yes, there were a lot of presents on that table, and yes, the room was filled with many people also holding presents, but not even a thank you? No excuse! It doesn't matter if the presents were being opened in the middle of Disneyland; how much time does it take to turn to the presenter of the gift and say thank you? And most importantly, to write a simple thank you card or note? When you put your mind to this one, writing a thank you note, letter, or card following the receipt of a gift of any kind will take a lot less time than it took to purchase the gift in the first place. A thank you note is the perfect expression that says the gift is appreciated, written to someone who has taken time out of their busy day to purchase or make a gift especially for you! One would think that the very least thing that could be offered in return is to take a few moments and express appreciation by just writing the words *thank you* on a note, card, or silly piece of paper, letting that person know that the gift and thoughtfulness were both appreciated. It must be the "think" part of this statement that is the problem. Any more, no one takes the time to think about writing a thank you note when a gift is received. And it seems to be a sure thing that no one is reaching back into those memory banks to allow that recorder to turn on—you remember, the one that has all of those lessons stored on proper etiquette, good manners, and common sense? A thank you note can make a world of difference in the gift-giving process and, without a doubt, is the proper and socially expected thing to do.

We can all agree that this is a fast and crazy world that we live in, and we are all very busy with projects, jobs, families, and, of course, friends. However, when a gift is received, we can also agree that at that very moment, we do experience the faint urge to say something like thank you, as the wrapping paper is torn away from the package, revealing the gift inside. But time and time again, in just seconds, the urge vanishes from our minds, the recorder stops, and there is nothing! No reply, no reaction at all, as if all of the time, emotion, and effort put forth in the selection of the gift had never taken place, and the gift had never been received, and the papers of yet another gift are well on the way to being torn off the next package, the cycle repeating itself.

Here is a question for you. Is just thinking about saying thank you or quietly mumbling the word *thanks* over the sounds of paper rattling and tissue rumbling a sufficient and proper thing to do? Is there a problem with that "think" thing again? Perhaps the proper question here should be, how long does it take to sit down and write a few words of appreciation for a gift that a friend, family member, or business coworker has put forth the time, love, and effort in selecting? Once again, figuring out the answer to this question should not take nearly as long as it took to purchase the gift, wrap it, and for that matter, not even as long as it would take to make yourself a snack and plant your body on the couch in front of the TV, and we all certainly make time for that. The answer to this question is a no-brainer, don't you agree?

The etiquette experts, parents, and teachers of the past and even of today, all stand firm on the fact that when a gift is received, the next step to follow is a properly written thank you note. It is not proper, or considerate for that matter, to assume that when a gift is received, the presenter of the gift automatically knows that the gift was great and appreciated, and no thank you is necessary, end of the story. Writing a thank you note, card, or letter does not take a lot of time, nor is it difficult, and that is a confirmed fact! So, when receiving a gift, a courtesy, or a favor of any kind, it is strongly suggested by social and by proper etiquette, that first, it is the social duty of the receiver of a gift to sit down and write a thank you card, note, or letter personally, to the giver of the gift, and second, it is the proper thing to do.

Receive a gift, write a thank you!

Redundant in print, but strong and direct in meaning. Get the point?

In chapter six, *When to Give a Gift*, there is a paragraph introducing the importance of a thank you, in gift or stationery form, given to a friend, a neighbor, or family member who has offered you a courtesy, favor, or gift. And, once again, the importance of a thank you was covered in the chapter

Gratuities or Tips, reminding us all about a handwritten note and a few words of appreciation for a job well-done or a service rendered on your behalf. So, as they say, the third time should be the charm.

A thank you note, card, or letter, handwritten and signed by the receiver and presented to the giver is always, without question, the following step to the receipt of any gift, suggested and outlined by both social and proper etiquette and the proper thing to do.

When a friend, family member, or neighbor helps out, a thank you note of appreciation is in order. When a friend has you over for dinner or takes you out to lunch, it is a perfect opportunity to say thank you with a note. Even though a thank you note or card is not wrapped up in pretty paper, nor topped with a fancy bow, it is considered a gift, personal and from the heart, and the handwritten message inside the note will make the gift even more special and will surely put a smile on the face of the receiver, just like opening a present.

Writing a thank you note each time a gift is presented, or when a courtesy or favor has been received is an etiquette rule that came to pass many centuries ago—a rule driven by the guidelines of social and proper etiquette, when the art of writing a thank you note was a socially mandatory step following the receipt of a favor or gift of any kind at any time. In today's busy world, writing a thank you note seems to be a proper step in good manners that most of us do not even think about unless it was taught and encouraged, beginning at a very early age. The basic rule of simple etiquette and good manners must begin early in life, taught by our parents or our mentors, and then passed down to our children, constantly encouraged and practiced without exception, each and every time a thank you note is in order.

Unfortunately, in the world of today, sitting down and writing a thank you note is a practice that most do not experience or partake in on a regular basis. Personally, I am from the old world of thinking, that when a gift, a courtesy, or a favor is received, it is first proper and next good manners, to recognize the gift or gesture with a written form of appreciation, and a handwritten thank you note is the perfect and proper manner to accomplish this duty.

It is surprising how many people do not have the slightest idea as to how to even write a thank you note. Lucky for you all, a simple and basic lesson on how to write a thank you note is on the next page; so let's get started.

The same *Simple Three—A, B, C* rule that applies to the creation of invitations and to announcements, also applies to a thank you in written form. The example of a basic thank you note is the same example that can be found in most all etiquette books. One that my family has followed for many years and the exact same example that was again re-taught to me in my sophomore year of high school business class a few years back; thank you, Mrs. Leonard. A simple and basic thank you note can be enhanced and personalized as you wish, but for now, a simple and basic example will get you on the proper track.

First: The introduction
Second: A personal and precise thank you for the favor or gift received
Third: An appropriate closing statement

Here is an example:

A. The introduction:

B. The body of the note:
This is a personal thank you so remember to thank the giver, in detail, for the courtesy or kindness that has been extended. Let the person know that the kindness has been noticed and appreciated and even add a few details if you wish.

C: Closing:
Complete the note of appreciation by using your own choice of words. Then a kind and proper last word and your name.

Dear Carson,

Thank you for the great model airplane. I am so excited to put the model together and hang it from the ceiling in my room. I saw this model in the toy store and really wanted it for my collection, and because of your kindness, now I have it.

When it is all finished, I would like you to come over and see my plane.

**Yours truly,
Ethan**

As you can see, it is very simple and doesn't take much time at all; but when the person who has extended a favor or courtesy, or who has given you a gift receives the thank you note, they will be pleased and quite possibly honored to be available to you in the future.

There is a shared opinion among those people who are not old world etiquette followers, that a thank you note is a waste of time and really not necessary. Well, you know what? In this very busy world, when every moment of the day is filled with a project, a pickup, or a duty, muttering the slang words, "hey, thanks, dude," just doesn't fill the bill. First of all, how many people do you know with the first name of *Hey* or *Dude*? Certainly not many, I hope! Remember another wise old saying that applies perfectly to the subject at hand, "Anything of value, will take time."

Take a few minutes to give these wise words some serious thought. My interpretation emphatically states that especially in this very busy world, anything, no, everything, that has value, will most certainly take time to achieve. This statement shows that we all must make a special effort in our busy and full schedules, to focus on the things of value—the important things. And if this is done, each time a favor or courtesy is extended or a gift is received, one will automatically stop and take a few minutes out of their day, to write a thank you note. The note may be short and sweet, but always detailed and to the point—and most importantly, it will be a true expression to the friend, neighbor, or family member that you do appreciate the favor, courtesy, or gift. It is amazing how powerful a thank you can be. That small gift can fill the room with joy, especially when the receiver accepts the note with a warm smile and a heart filled with satisfaction, knowing that the offer of goodness or gift was appreciated by you.

The Simple Three—A, B, C on a card, note, or on a piece of paper, personally handwritten, says thank you. And, surprise, it only takes a few minutes. As an adult, a thank you note for a model plane will probably not be the case, but you get the idea; improvise and use the same *Simple Three*—A, B, C form whether it is a child thanking a friend for a model airplane or an adult thanking a business associate for an excellent bottle of vintage red wine.

And remember that a thank you note, card, or letter must always be written immediately following the receipt of any gift. Think of it as homework, a chore, or a job that is expected to be accomplished each time a gift is received. A page of math or a household chore must be done in a timely manner and turned in or mailed to the appropriate person in a specific time frame. When you put this piece of homework in the to-do pile, it will never get done. Things come up, time passes, and this very important piece of homework is buried in the "get-around-to-it" box and forever forgotten. A thank you note should be written as soon as the gift is received—not the exact minute that it is opened, but by the end of the next day, because when the excitement of the gift is still fresh in your mind, that excitement can be put in words in a thank you note, card, or letter and expressed with enthusiasm to the person who selected the gift especially for you. Take the time to offer the same courtesy that you received when a friend, family member, or business associate shopped, wrapped, and trimmed a gift for you; the next step is writing a thank you note, expressing just how much the gift meant to you. Make a not-so-messy snack—something that you can munch on—or pour yourself a nice cup of coffee and enjoy a sip while you are writing the thank you note. Sit down at the table with one hand holding a pen and the other handling the munchies or the coffee cup. With the TV still in full sight, you can conquer two dragons with one sword in one fatal swoop. Writing the thank you note, card, or letter is the first dragon that will make that special someone feel very important, and enjoying the snack or cup of coffee along with the TV program of your choice, will be conquering dragon number two. With a little help from the fridge, a fresh pot of coffee, and the TV, there can no longer be any excuse for not getting a thank you note, card, or letter taken care of in a timely manner.

There are a few proper etiquette rules for sending a thank you, with a possible variance with each occasion. But make no mistake, although the variance will be in the time frame allowed for the thank you to be sent, the importance of writing a thank you immediately following the receipt of the gift still applies across the board.

Holiday or special event gifts: Social and proper etiquette says that a thank you note, card, or letter should be written and mailed within two weeks after receiving the gift. Sooner is always better!

Following a holiday, stationery stores and cards shops all have delightful and appropriate thank you stationery that can be purchased. After the holidays, the holiday stationery is all on sale! If you do not have, or wish to purchase, specific holiday card stock, your personal stationery will do nicely.

Wedding gifts: Social etiquette says that there is a six month to one year time frame allowed for the mailing of a thank you note, card, or letter. However, proper etiquette and common sense says that even six months can be an eternity, especially if the presenter of the gift is waiting with bated breath to receive some type of written acknowledgement that the item, selected with love and care, was appreciated. With that in mind, it is suggested that upon receipt of a wedding gift, which is in most cases, prior to the wedding date, a thank you note is written, personally and with precise detail referring to the gift received, as per the example above. Then the thank you note is held in a safe place to be mailed following the wedding. Suggested mailing time frame is within one month of the wedding date. Remember that as a wedding gift is given in honor and celebration of a wedding, the thank you for the gift, although often received prior to the wedding day, is not mailed until after the wedding has taken place.

The thank you note for a wedding gift, also referred to as the *informal*, is often ordered at the same time as the wedding invitation stationery. The thank you note can be created using the same card stock, ink, and fonts as the wedding invitation, and when ordered at the same time, along with the mailing envelope, can be more cost efficient. Usually it is suggested that the number of thank you notes or informal cards should be ordered in a larger quantity than the invitations as the thank yous can be used for years to come, if created properly. A suggested 50 percent addition for the thank you notes is a good amount—not too few and not too many.

Thank you notes or informal cards can also be purchased elsewhere, following the order of your wedding invitations; the choice is up to you. First and foremost in mind must be simply that a gift has been received and a handwritten thank you must follow, so choose the thank you note stationery properly. An old and valuable lesson from years gone by, that should be taught to children all the way through adulthood, and encouraged on every occasion of gift giving by parents, mentors, and teachers, is that when a gift is received, a thank you note must follow.

A few years ago, I had the pleasure of working with a family on a very unique wedding. This family was one of the kindest and most thoughtful families I had ever had the experience of dealing with; one that will hold a special place in my heart for years to come. The story begins with a telephone call from the father. There were seven children in the family, all boys except one special daughter, who was getting married. She was a lovely young lady who ultimately made the most beautiful and gracious bride. During the orchestration of this very special event, I had the opportunity to meet the youngest member of the family, a little boy in first grade, if memory serves me correctly, with a very vivid imagination and a delightfully animated manner of expressing himself. If only his energy could be bottled and sold. A few months into the planning, this little man announced that he was having a surgery that would keep him off his feet for several weeks. When I heard the news, of course, the social and proper etiquette lessons automatically popped in my head, and I went shopping. A bag of crayons, coloring books, clay and other busy little boy items were purchased then assembled in a gift bag, then stuffed with colorful and happy tissue. A suitable card was attached to the bag and finished with a brightly colored big bow. The busy bag was then given to Mom to take home to my new little friend. In a very short and most timely manner, I received a bright green envelope addressed to me personally, AVA, no last name, just AVA. When I opened the envelope, a giant Barney-like dinosaur with the words "thank you" jumped out at me, and I realized that this little man, no doubt with the assistance and encouragement from Mom, had handwritten inside, "Thank you for my gift. Love, Tommy."

My heart filled with joy and the biggest smile I had produced in months came over my face as I looked at the silly dinosaur and enjoyed the wonderful first grader's penmanship on the card—a thank you written especially for me for a simple courtesy that was extended. The end of the story, stating truly and sincerely, that a written expression of thanks can brighten up anyone's day. It certainly added sunshine to mine.

Chapter Eleven

Remember the Personal Letter?

YEARS AGO, A specific form of stationery was the only means of correspondence, personally and professionally, and was the main course of communication. This form of correspondence and communication was called a letter. A letter is a written form of contact, correspondence, and communication with family, friends, and business associates near and far away. The telephone was not yet discovered and when Mr. Alexander Graham Bell did complete this ingenious invention, allowing folks a more efficient and faster form of communication, the availability to a family was costly and it was not readily available across the land; therefore, the art of letter writing continued.

Today, can you imagine the world without a telephone in the kitchen to make a call to a friend when preparing a meal, or a wireless phone in the family room or den, to chat or text while watching a favorite TV program?

Imagine a world with no Internet service to send messages back and forth with friends and family or to attend to business dealings. Handwritten letters were depended upon to carry messages across the land to those who were special, to those we wanted to keep in touch with, and to those we were working on business ventures with.

Think about it—a world with no computers to replace the writing method of hand and pen to paper.

Most of us, including me, would not survive without the modern day conveniences of telephones, internet, texting, and computers, not to mention FedEx, UPS, and Priority Mail to expedite letters and packages. But not so long ago, the most commonly used form of communicating with families and friends was writing a letter to keep up with the happenings of the world and to share special times and emotions with loved ones and business associates; these letters were handwritten, putting pen and ink to paper, using the same *Simple Three—A, B, C* rule that we use today in invitations, announcements, and thank you notes.

Years ago, letters were written on paper—often family-milled—or on fabric or even on pieces of wood. Today, stationery materials have evolved considerably and can be purchased at a number of different types of stores. Stationery materials are offered in many colors, paper weights, and card stocks that can be used in stationery form. And now the many forms of stationery can be personalized with monograms, engravings, embossing, and letter pressings. Ink colors are offered in every shade imaginable, and the very popular "*bling*," such as crystals, pearls, beading, and jewels are also available for the asking. Wonderful, fun, and proper forms of writing materials with matching envelopes, which can be used for writing letters, for thank you cards, for invitations, and announcements, personally and professionally, are all easily available in today's busy world.

Invitations, announcements, a thank you, or a letter to a friend and all other forms of stationery should all follow the *Simple Three—A, B, C* steps and social and proper etiquette guidelines of why, when, and how to write any form of stationery in good taste: simple basic rules that should be followed by each and every person, every day in every way.

Stenographers, secretaries, and assistants still use a note pad when taking dictation or instructions from their employer. Young ladies are still keeping diaries, documenting the most secret and special thoughts and emotions experienced throughout the day. And authors, screenwriters, and poets still turn to their journals or index cards, to jot down ideas for their next bestseller, blockbuster, or collection: all forms of stationery to be used, properly and respectively, and later to be shared with friends, family, and business associates in very important ways.

Chapter Twelve

Social Gatherings

THE TITLE OF *Social Gatherings* alone can open the door to a very large and powerful etiquette avalanche, beginning with expected proper behavior and continuing through the suggested Six O'clock Rules, with many stops in between. So once again, let's begin by saying that in life "there is a time and a place for everything," a rule that plays heavily on the topic of social gatherings.

As for expected proper behavior at a social gathering, this should be an easy one. Proper behavior means behaving properly—to display appropriate actions applicable to any given situation or setting, expressing courtesy, good manners, and a presentation of total self-control by acting in a responsible and acceptable manner. This is not to say that when we are enjoying a night out with our family or friends, we cannot get a bit rowdy and have fun. On the contrary, it simply suggests that we display our fun and excitement in a manner that is comfortable for everyone around us—a manner so in the morning, we can all look in the mirror and not feel ashamed or embarrassed about something that happened the night before. There is more that falls under the title *Social Gatherings*, such as the proper use of words and chewing gum. How about cell phones ringing in the middle of a restaurant or during the SAT tests? And the Six O'clock Rules—what are they? The best approach to learning about any topic is to learn the definition of a topic. The meaning of any topic is the open door to the subject; so let's begin with the meaning of *social gatherings*.

There are two words introducing this topic. Once again, after consulting Mr. Webster for his opinion: *social* means "living or organized in a community;

not solitary; relating to human beings living in society; sociable." And *gathering* is defined as "a meeting or crowd of people; a collection of people or objects."

So *social* means to be and or live with others, not alone.

And *gathering* means a group of people or objects.

Together, a *social gathering* is more than one person gathering together in one place or group. Agreed? And just like any subject, there are rules and guidelines that are suggested by social or proper etiquette or simple common sense, to ensure that the gathering is a pleasant and sociable get-together. The guidelines suggested by this topic are offered by both social and proper etiquette and are simple and easy to follow; they are also directed by our old friends, common sense and simple grace. Social gatherings can be a group of friends going to the movie or a hundred guests sitting in a ballroom enjoying a wonderful meal in celebration of a marriage. A social gathering can be a group of friends at a football game. Whatever the occasion, when the gathering includes more than one person, it is considered a social gathering and following a few simple rules can ensure that everyone has a great time.

Chapter Thirteen

Using the Proper Word

OH, THE STORIES that have been shared while sitting with friends and family by the neighborhood swimming pool, or in front of a raging fire on the beach. Stories filled with fact often dosed heavily with fiction and most likely laced with a variety of great words that, at the time, sounded appropriate for the story, but when looking back at the situation, made absolutely no sense at all. Not to worry—it happens to everyone, and help is on the way.

Using the proper word at the proper time seems to be a rarity rather than a common practice as we, the partakers in the sport of people watching, experience more often than not. The usage of an improper word is like frozen ice chips sliding down one's back, sending chills throughout one's body, and, hence, a subject that must be covered.

We are all guilty of this proper etiquette error from time to time, but when we hear an improper word being used in a conversation or sentence by others, or just during casual chitchat with our friends, we all react in a similar manner. A strange feeling creeps into our body, the same feeling as if we were sitting in a classroom and chalk is screeching down the chalkboard, or when we first jump into a cold river or lake, making our bodies shiver.

Most often, people use improper words because they do not take the time to learn the meaning of the word, or discover new words to increase their vocabulary. The result is usually a word pulled out of the sky and used wherever it seems to fit, proper or not. This method of communicating is not a safe or intelligent path to follow for anyone, because if a word, any word, is just randomly pulled from the sky and slipped into a sentence to fill the space, usually the word is not the correct one that should be used. Solution? Make a game out of learning new words or the meaning of words that you are not certain about. We all love games!

When a new word is heard or when you are in need of a new word to assist in the explanation of a topic you are trying to share, or as support in expressing yourself, it is your responsibility to find out the proper meaning of the word well before the word is used. Visit Mr. Webster, or *DK Illustrated Oxford,* or any dictionary you may have, and do some research. Ask a parent, a family member, or a teacher if there is a question about the meaning of a word. The answers are all readily available, and all that needs to be done is just look it up or ask! When you discover a new word, or the correct meaning of a word you have heard a million times before but were not sure what it meant, the doors open and that perfect opportunity is before you.

Use the word in a proper sentence. Apply it properly with forethought and understanding. Then file the word in your memory bank for future use.

The power of words—understanding their meaning and having the ability to use the words in proper sentences—enables you to grow by expanding your vocabulary, which will open new doors to opportunities along the way. The more words you have in your daily vocabulary, the broader your street of travel becomes and the greater your destination will be. There is no ceiling on the amount of words you are allowed; the sky is the limit, and all of the words that you use are the stars. Fill the galaxy of your world with as many words as your memory bank can hold and enjoy the journey. Have fun with the knowledge and experience and the rewards of a full and vast vocabulary by adding new words and their meanings to your memory bank every day. And as you travel through life, listen to the words that are spoken to you and around you and then decide for yourself if the word game is working for you. When asked if this game is a keeper, my reply is a big *YES*! It works, and it works well. When a child uses or pronounces a word incorrectly, we all get a chuckle out of it and may say, "Isn't that cute?" But when an adult blurts out a blatant improperly, or mispronounced word or makes a grammatical error, there is not a chuckle to be heard—and I prefer not to comment on what may be said.

The moral to this story is that a wise man thinks about what he is going to say before he says anything. Good moral, don't you agree? Think first, then speak the word. It is the thinking part that allows the recorders in our mind to kick in and start working so that the proper word can be chosen. Many of history's most brilliant people are recognized for taking time to think before speaking. Carefully select the proper words before they are spoken. Taking the time to find the appropriate word and knowing the proper and correct meaning of the word, and then speaking it, is what will make the difference—the difference in expressing intelligence and knowledge, while displaying good manners at the same time.

Opening your mouth before thinking and allowing whatever to pop out, can often be the gateway into an embarrassing situation; it is usually followed by an expected and lengthy explanation of why anyone would use *that* particular word and, in turn, may invite the question, "Did you really mean to say that?" If a word pops into your head and you really are not confident in the meaning of the word, don't use it! Take a few seconds, dig a little deeper into that memory bank, and pull out the word that will express exactly what you mean, one that you are sure of—or visit a dictionary and discover a new word, a correct word that can be used with confidence. Never just use a word because it may sound impressive, as it is a sure thing that the word is probably not the word that should be used.

When in doubt, don't use the word!

Words, old and new, are like little presents that are powerful and free of charge: one of the few presents that when received, does not mandate a thank you note or an explanation of where it came from. The gift of words, when received and fully understood, belongs to you from that moment forward. Words are given to you with no strings attached, but there is a silent requirement to owning words—the meaning of the word must be learned, and then used properly and as often as possible.

In my generation, it was very common to play word games at home and at school. My father, my very dearest friend's father, as well as teachers at school, would often ask that we all look up or choose a word, any word, find out its meaning by doing a little homework, and the next day, use the new word in sentences as many times as we could. Now, I ask you to stimulate the old brain cells by doing the same thing. You may be surprised how responsive those little brain cells will be. When a word has been possessed by learning its proper spelling, discovering its meaning, and using the word throughout an entire day by writing and saying it over and over again, the feeling of satisfaction is amazing! Choose another word the next day and the word game continues. Consistency is the key to all knowledge—just another one of those wise sayings that we have all heard time and time again.

New words can be obtained in many ways. Sometimes the word can be given to you by someone during a conversation. Perhaps reading the word in a newspaper, book, or on the chalkboard at school will be the introduction. Wherever the word comes from, the rules to the game remain the same.

Learn the correct spelling of the word.

Learn the proper meaning of the word.

Use the new word throughout the day as often as possible.

File the word in your memory bank.

Your memory bank will continue to grow as your vocabulary grows. No, I was not a bored little girl growing up trying to find different things to occupy my time, and there is no giggling allowed here, as I can imagine a few of you thinking that if I wasn't bored then I must have totally lost my mind to turn learning into a game. Quite the contrary!

This game of discovering words and their meanings was fun and exciting: a surprising and new adventure to partake in each day, and the most incredible way to increase your vocabulary with only a little bit of effort. Finding and using new words was a challenge, and the grand prize was all yours. I must admit, even my brother, who was not fond of school, actually enjoyed participating in this word game and had a very good time playing it. It is a simple and fun method of expanding one's vocabulary, experienced while playing a game, as well as a sure way of stimulating the old brain cells and allowing oneself a form of expression with confidence—we all can benefit from that. It is never too late, nor is anyone ever too old to play the word game. Just give it a try! You may be surprised as to how exciting it is to hear and learn new words. Not slang words or ones that cannot be repeated in crowds, especially when Mom and Dad are around. Learn the good words and the meaning of the good words, then use and apply the words to everyday life, expanding dreams along the way. New words that can be included in conversations with friends, with family, and with teachers and at the same time can increase one's vocabulary. Great words can introduce all kinds of exciting adventures. There is no time like the present to begin the word game with your child or with your friends. It is a game that can be taught to and played with anyone, anywhere, and in turn, applied at any time. It is a very simple game that can open doors to the future and answer questions of the past, precisely and properly. And the reward is that all words can be owned by you. Thousands of words and their meanings can be yours by simply learning the proper spelling and meaning and then applying the word each day. I have never been a school teacher, but I do believe that words are power and when you have them, the world is then your oyster!

Chapter Fourteen

Silence—A Good Thing?

IF THIS QUESTION were asked of the teacher of a third-grade class, on a clear and sunny day just before the bell was scheduled to ring announcing that school is out for the summer, I can honestly say that the teacher would answer yes, at that moment, silence would be a wonderful thing! But, in many social situations, silence can be misunderstood as rude or even disrespectful to those around you, not to mention an expression of inappropriate behavior.

Let's say that you are having dinner with friends, and everyone is sitting around the dining table. Or a few friends are sitting around the swimming pool shooting the breeze, and the person sitting next to you, possibly your date, stands up and disappears without a word.

This form of silence—not communicating—is not proper, nor is it acceptable, and it is considered socially rude, very rude. A simple, "excuse me" or even a cool "hey, I'll be right back," is more polite than just standing up and disappearing into space, without saying a word. Silence in this situation would be considered improper, or bluntly put, bad manners, and, unfortunately, is displayed all of the time by young and old alike.

I actually presented a question regarding the disappearing act to a member of our family. I would also like to add that with the exception of this one offered trait, this family member is the most kind and loving person imaginable, with very good manners, so the disappearing act was a puzzler. Following my question to this family member, the excuse that was given to me was, "I was just getting a glass of water and assumed that you knew I was going to be right back."

I promptly replied, "Assume? No, I didn't assume, nor do I ever assume anything!" We all know very well what the word "assume" means, and whether the disappearing act precedes a visit to the kitchen, or a trip to the moon, do not assume that anyone else will know where you are going without a brief explanation. Open your mouth and say, "excuse me," before you get up from a table or as you leave a space in the presence of others. Where you are going is your business; when you leave a space without a word, it becomes everyone's business. A few little words letting the others know that you will be right back is all that is required. Jumping up and vanishing into thin air, leaving everyone thinking that you were totally bored with their company or were abducted by space aliens, is impolite and improper. Stand up and excuse yourself; it will only take a minute and is the socially expected thing to do.

Taking the silence thing a step further would be when one is asked a question and there is no reply. Silence is never the suggested reply. When one has taken the time and extended the effort to ask a question, one must in turn reply with an answer. Simply open your mouth and use your words. If you do not have any words, quickly find them and reply verbally, hopefully in some form of intelligent manner. A short and sweet reply is acceptable, and a simple reply is better than no reply at all. Never reply to a question with silence; do not just sit there like a lump on a log and say nothing. Silence as a reply to a question is rude and strongly implies disrespect to the people around you, saying that they really are not important enough to justify a reply. No one enjoys being ignored, especially when a question is asked. Not responding to a question asked, followed by complete silence, is like a double strike in a less-than-desirable ballgame—a double strike that results in three strikes, you're out! Alright, a little dramatic, but nevertheless, being silent at an inappropriate time is not well received. On the other hand, silence at bedtime for children, is peaceful. And silence while watching a movie or TV program is enjoyable. Silence when someone else is talking, and it is not your turn to talk, is considered polite.

Recently I have become friends with a gentleman who could be considered a *facilitator of conversation*. He is a great listener of conversation, absorbing each and every word and then processing those words into meaning. Did I mention that this friend *facilitates conversation* in complete silence and with no reaction or sign of acknowledgment that anyone else is even in the room? Oftentimes I have been guilty of chatting away on the phone with him, then after moments of dead silence, asking if he is still with me. Is my newfound friend being rude? No, not rude, but it would be nice if some sort of reaction by words or action was offered and it certainly would eliminate the question entirely of "rude or not rude." Even a single word of acknowledgment would verify that your words are being heard. A nod of the head or a simple smile can also offer assurance that your words are not being ignored. Silence can be mistaken for rudeness; reaction even in its most simplistic manner can make the difference.

Chapter Fifteen

The Six O'clock Candle

THERE IS AN etiquette rule that simply states, when using candles as a form of lighting, ambience, or illumination, never light the candle before six o'clock in the evening. The etiquette experts of long ago, Post, Vanderbilt, and even Miss Manners touched on this rule, which was followed without question. In today's world, it is ignored. My feeling on this rule is that one should fall back on good common sense and honor this rule for practical reasons. During the day, prior to six o'clock in the evening, the sun is shining, so there is no need for candles, is there? If candles are lit and the sun is shining, can they even be seen? It is unlikely! So when in doubt, ask, and the question is solved. Ask an event professional; ask the proprietor of the candle shop– they should have the answer. If not, ask an etiquette professional or refer to reference books on the subject and you will find the answer. And if you cannot find an event professional, the candle shop is closed, the etiquette professionals are engaged, and you can't find your glasses to read from a reference book on the subject, then fall back on good common sense. During the day, the area can depend on the sun for light. After six o'clock in the evening, the natural light is usually no longer available so other sources of light are needed. Hence, the use of candlelight.

There are many uses for candles. Candles can be a source of romance, or an inviting fragrance in one's home. They can be an accent piece of décor, or a faux sense of a summer bouquet of fresh flowers, or any other fragrance one wishes to simulate. Candles can present an illusion of a home-baked pie with the magic of the burning flame enriching the surrounding space. And candles can set the mood for a special occasion. Candles can be used to light or illuminate a table space while enjoying a perfect meal. A candle has many uses, but one must remember that when candles are used, the six o'clock rule should be followed. The six o'clock candle rule states that candles should not be lit before six o'clock in the evening. Here are some various situations where candles are commonly used. How does the rule apply:

Lighting votive candles on a dining table, or candlesticks at a restaurant or social event? No, not before six o'clock.

Decorating a wedding chapel with hurricane candles that line the pathway of an aisle introducing the entrance of the bridal party? No, not before six o'clock.

Using encased or open-flame candles at a gathering at home or on a country club dining table; candles, including scented candles, lit and placed in a room creating romantic ambience light and fragrance? No, and no, not before six o'clock. Before six o'clock in the evening, natural light should still be available in most parts of the world. After six o'clock in the evening, most often the natural light is gone and other sources of light, such as candles, can illuminate the surroundings and highlight their beauty.

Here's another one for you. You are having company drop by after the big game. The kids' soccer socks were shoved under the bed without anyone's knowledge or Dad's basketball shirt was tossed in the closet for the third time without seeing the inside of the washer, both sharing a definite fragrance that is not quite up to snuff. Oh, almost forgot, it is late afternoon, three-thirty to be precise. What do you do?

Most people would reach for the can of room spray or light a candle, a scented candle, and the fragrance of the candle would quickly engulf the entire house as if there were flowers blooming in the center of the living room, or as if Mom had just pulled a homemade pumpkin or spiced apple pie out of the oven. Yum! But is this the proper thing to do?

What if you are a real estate agent selling a house that smells "stale" because it has been closed up for some time? Do you light an air-freshening candle to send flower fragrance into the air?

Following the six o'clock candle rule, the proper thing to do is to light the scented candle and let it burn for perhaps fifteen or twenty minutes before the expected arrival of your guests. Then, just before the open house begins or guests walk through the front door, blow the candle out! Yes, blow the flame of the candle out, leaving only the fragrance of the scented candle to continue permeating the space for hours, eliminating any embarrassment or explanation for a candle burning. The unidentifiable odors have been blanketed and only the fragrance of the once-lit candle will be left behind. One warning on the faux edible scented candle trick: if the scented candle that has been selected is the homemade pie candle, you may wish to make a market run and pick up a pie before the guests arrive or you may have to explain why the goodies are not being shared.

If you follow the six o'clock rule, there will not be a need to explain a lit candle in the middle of the afternoon should any of the guests own an etiquette book.

It's common sense; if the candle remains lit, there will be some explaining to do. Rarely is it dark at three-thirty in the afternoon so one certainly does not need candlelight. An obvious assumption upon seeing a lit candle prior to six o'clock in the evening would be a cover-up—stirring the pot, so to speak, in the minds of the guests. We all are familiar with the active imaginations of people. Perhaps there was the lingering scent of a basketball game with the guys or the entire team when dirty socks were left in the laundry basket or hidden in the closet. Maybe there are pets and the cleanup duties were completely forgotten. And there is always the bad cooking trail, revealing that a prepared meal was tossed into the garbage can because no one remembered to stir the pot. The solution is the six o'clock candle rule, or for now, the common sense rule, is to pull a scented candle out of the cupboard and light it, allowing the fragrance of the candle to fill the room and mask the charred smell of the pot roast. Then, before the open house or moments before the guests walk in the door, destroy the evidence by blowing out the scented candle and enjoy the compliments of the fragrance that is left behind. No explanations are needed because the six o'clock candle rule has been honored. No embarrassment, and no distasteful odors to feed the imaginations of the guests, because the flame of the candle has been extinguished and the only thing that is left behind is a clean and fresh scent—just a little tip that has been provided by proper etiquette and good old common sense over the years.

We have touched on the six o'clock rule with regard to candles and now have a pretty good idea why candles should not be used before six for any form of lighting. Like most rules, there is, of course, an exception simply stating that candles can be used prior to six o'clock in the evening when used in a church, temple, or synagogue, or as part of a religious ceremony. Now, I don't wish to dive into the mode of wedding planner on this subject, however, a good example to this exception on the six o'clock candle rule is the lighting of a unity candle during a wedding ceremony.

With a *unity candle lighting*, usually there is an arrangement of some sort, holding three candles, or one large candle with three wicks. The side candles, or wicks, are called the family candles. A member from the bride's family and a member of the groom's family will approach the unity arrangement and light their appropriate candles. Lighting the family candles symbolizes permission, or a blessing given by the family to the couple to join the families together as one—the *unity*. The center candle is considered the couple's candle. The bride and groom take the flame from their family candles and together light a center candle, uniting the entire family as one, resulting in a single flame burning as one.

There is also a *memory candle lighting* whereby the flame of a candle is the symbol in memory of a loved one, perhaps at a time of loss or illness. In some churches or temples, on birthdays and holidays, and during difficult times, memory candles are lit throughout the day and night, by a friend or family member signifying that the memory of a loved one is recognized. This form of candle lighting, or prayer for a loved one, says that the memory of the loved one will burn brightly forever. There are also birthday candles; one candle lit in honor of each year celebrated. Candles that are placed on a cake then lit and at that Kodak moment with one huff and puff, the birthday wish is granted as the flame of the birthday candles are blown out.

The six o'clock candle rule of when or when not to light a candle has been a thing of the past for many years; but now the rule on candles is clear, and you are an authority on the subject. And as an authority, you can share the knowledge with friends and family. Assist in the lighting of candles or blowing them out, because when one puts some thought into this rule, it is a sensible rule that can be followed easily—a rule guided by etiquette hand-in-hand with good common sense.

Chapter Sixteen

Chewing Gum

THERE ARE MANY reasons for chewing gum: jaw exercise, breath freshener, to assist in curbing one's appetite, and of course, because it looks cool. Chewing gum for some people is a substitute for habits, such as smoking or eating. In fact, there is a nicotine substitute for smoking in a gum form.

The issue here is not the chewing of gum; it is the manner in which it is chewed, and in many cases, where one chooses to take part in this act. Once again, "there is a time and a place for everything" comes into play with this habit. There are suggested rules outlined by proper etiquette, hand-in-hand with good manners and common sense, that can assist in making the right decision as to when and where gum chewing is acceptable.

Have you ever been at a meeting or at school, and from across the room, for some reason, a person has caught your eye? And, as if the entire picture is in full screen, all you see are jaws chomping up and down, and all you hear is the popping of gum being tossed back and forth in a larger-than-life cavity that is a mouth.

Or how about when you are seated at a ceremony site and the sounds of beautiful classical music fill the air, announcing the entrance of the bride. All of the guests turn toward the end of the aisle, all eyes on this vision of beauty dressed in white, and like a needle bursting a bubble, the happy smile that you think you are looking at on the face of the lovely bride is really a big wad of bubble gum, and the music that is now floating through the air includes the sounds of the bride's jaw chomping up and down as she makes her way to the waiting groom. Now *this* is a Kodak moment!

Chewing gum may be acceptable in the proper setting, and when chewed in a proper manner, although I really can't think of any at this time. But I can say that chewing gum is never acceptable in public with an open mouth, sharing all of the wonderful sounds of chomp, pop, chomp—at any time. The sound effects of chewing gum should really be added to the list of social taboos because, honestly, no one really wants to share this experience with anyone.

Chewing gum should never be acceptable at school, and, believe it or not, there are some schools, public and private alike, that enforce this rule with detention or some form of punishment. Not empty words—just a fact!

Chewing gum is never acceptable at a social event. Can anyone honestly say while enjoying an opera, that they truly believe that the sound effects of chomping gum are welcome?

I think not!

And there is always the question of what to do with that wad of gum when it is time to sit down at the table and enjoy a wonderful meal or when the jaw exercise session is over. Is it proper to unload the gum into a napkin? No! The napkin could be fabric, and don't even think about hiding a sticky glob of gum on or under the table. Not acceptable at any time!

Chewing gum is never acceptable in a professional setting either. I have worked my entire adult life and can say with complete commitment that I do not ever remember having an employer encourage gum chewing in the workplace. Answering a telephone call or sharing ideas around a conference table with a wad of gum popping back and forth in an open mouth, will not invite a promotion in the near future, nor will it make any positive statements about an employee or on an employer's behalf.

You know, when it comes right down to the nitty-gritty of chewing gum, there really is not an appropriate time or place to chew gum other than in the privacy of one's own home or in one's own space, because it seems that when chewing gum, we all seem to forget that it should be done in the same manner as chewing food—with one's mouth closed, and please, no sound effects!

Chapter Seventeen

Cell Phones

NOW HERE IS another bone of contention that seems to pop up in many conversations, and is a real sore spot for many, especially me.

The topic of a cell phone.

Most professional people, including me, now own and depend on a cell phone or form of a cell phone to survive. A great many kids and adults own and depend on a cell phone for one reason or another. Once again, the statement "there is a time and a place for everything" applies to the cell phone situation. I must also say that it is unbelievable how many kids and adults alike are oblivious to this statement! There really *is* a time and a place for the use of a cell phone, and with sincere hope, someday this fact will be a part of life for every person who owns and depends on a cell phone.

Picture this—moving back to the wedding day: the perfect location has been selected to share the wedding vows with the person of your dreams. The guests have arrived and are seated properly on the heavily carved, dark oak pews, the people on the left and right sides of the church anxiously awaiting the arrival of the bride. The center aisle is lined with lavish bouquets of cascading flowers, fragrant and full of colors that compliment the couple's personal taste. In the center of each floral cluster, a candle stands proudly, encased in etched glass, reflecting a romantic glow throughout the entire building. From the balcony behind the last row of oak pews, a string quartet is performing Pachelbel's *Canon in D Major,* and the glow from the altar candles twinkles as if they are inviting the ceremony to begin.

Following a moment's pause, the few notes of music flow lightly, announcing the entrance of the bride. The guests all stand to catch a glimpse of this vision of beauty who is now walking through the doorway and…it happens! The space is filled with the ringing of a cell phone, shattering the vision, along with the mood.

Someone forgot to turn off his or her cell phone!

Again, there is a time and a place for everything and a cell phone has no place at a wedding. No place at a reception, at a restaurant, or in a movie theater. A cell phone has no place at any social gathering because the ringing of the cell phone is disruptive, inconsiderate, and rude to everyone in the space surrounding the owner of the cell phone. If a cell phone is the lifeline to one's livelihood, or you, as a parent, are expecting a call from a child, be considerate, turn off the ringer on the phone and turn it to the vibrate setting. The vibration will still be heard, but is far less disruptive than the blare of a ringing phone. When the call comes in, fewer people will be aware of the incoming call and the receiver of the call will feel his or her pocket or purse wiggle. The ideal and most respectful solution is to turn the phone off or not bring the cell phone at all. But if you must receive an incoming call, get up quietly and respectively, and walk completely away from any surrounding guests, moving into a private place before you begin speaking. You will be able to take the call without anyone sitting or standing around you. Quite frankly, no one is really interested in sharing your conversation. Even if you are out shopping, in a grocery market, at the mall, or in a specialty shop, turn off the ringer on the cell phone and set it to vibrate, ensuring that when an incoming call comes through, you and only you can sense the call and respond to the vibration in your pocket or purse, walking away from any surrounding guests.

Another annoying issue regarding a cell phone is the yelling! I don't understand why when one is talking on a cell phone, the voice expands in volume and the yelling begins. When a call is answered on a cell phone, speak quietly, directly into the receiver. Why does a person answering a cell phone insist on screaming into the receiver during the entire conversation? If you have difficulty hearing, push the little volume button on the side of the cell phone and increase the volume for your ears only. There is no need to scream into the receiver and share unwelcome conversations with the world around you. As for the level of your voice, please take it down a few notches. As we parents say to our children, *use your inside voice* or *your quiet voice* when talking on a cell phone or any phone.

Did you know that in December of 2009, Wikipedia posted on Google that in the United States, 91 percent of the population were mobile phone users? Honestly! I also read an article in a newspaper about this and, of course, confirmed the statistic by surfing the Web, and it really was not a surprise, taking into consideration all of the great deals offered by cell phone companies backed by advertisement after advertisement, by mailings, on TV, and in magazines—everyone can own one! And here is something else to keep in mind: where there is ownership, there is responsibility, and the same etiquette and common sense rules apply to the use of a cell phone as they do to talking on a landline and those rules are as follows:

1. When talking on a telephone, any type of phone, be considerate of those around you. No one in the space surrounding a person on the phone is really interested in the phone conversation.
2. If you are engaged socially, professionally, or personally, a cell phone should be turned off, allowing the call to go into voicemail or be answered by a message service. Then, when free or disengaged, pick up the messages and return the calls in a timely manner.
3. If you are expecting a professional or family member call that demands immediate attention, turn the ringer off and the vibrate option on. When the call comes in, excuse yourself from the social space for a moment and take the call.
4. Always remember to use your inside voice, quietly and respectively.

It is time for just one more little question, promise! I have shared how I personally feel about the improper use of cells phones; do I stand alone on this subject? How do you feel? Here's the scenario:

Approximately 200 people are attending a seminar at the corporate offices of a major insurance company; all are professionals and all depend on their cell phones to keep them up to date on all of the new information. The president of a worldwide company is the key speaker, and although his presentation is interesting, it has been in session for three hours and everyone is getting restless. The lady seated next to you continues to look at her cell phone and within moments, her phone begins to ring, loudly! What is the proper thing for her to do?

A. Before entering the seminar, turn the phone off and when there is a break or intermission, move away from the group and pick up the message on the voice mail.
B. Quickly answer the call and carry on a conversation with the person on the other end of the phone in a less-than-inside voice?
C. Quickly answer the call, put the call on speaker phone so everyone can hear the conversation, because everyone is looking at her anyway.

The correct answer is A: Before entering the seminar, turn the phone off and when there is a break or intermission, move away from the group and pick up the message on voice mail. The answer to this question is simple and based on good common sense. It is not considerate to even enter the seminar space knowing that your cell phone may ring, disturbing everyone within the space.

Chapter Eighteen

And You Are?

UNINVITED GUESTS ARE another topic that hits close to home, personally as well as professionally. For some unexplained reason, when an invitation to a social event is extended to friends, family members, and business associates, the mistaken interpretation of the single name on the envelope or the personal call to one individual, is that everyone is invited, and that is usually not the case.

Let's do a little backtracking on this one. First, socially, if a guest is invited to an event, the guest name will be written on the invitation. If there is no name on the invitation, he or she is not invited! It's as simple as that. Never assume that it is acceptable to bring a guest if there is no invitation for an additional guest. Make sense? If you are a newly engaged or a recently married person and an invitation was received prior to this personal commitment, and the invitation is extended to you and you would like to bring this special person to the event, contact the sender of the invitation, share the good news of the engagement or recent marriage with the inviter, and then personally ask if it would be acceptable to bring this person with you. Never assume that it will be all right without asking and just arrive with an uninvited guest, special or not. Chances are more likely than not that this unannounced arrival will create some scrambling around by the host/hostess to accommodate your act of disrespect to the inviter. Yes, I did say disrespect. To assume that a single invitation can be extended to anyone other than the person whose name is on the invitation, without confirming with the inviter if bringing an additional guest would be alright, is an act of disrespect. And taking this a step further, if, as parents, you have accepted an invitation to an event and the words "family" or the family members specific names are not written on the invitation, you must confirm that it is acceptable with the inviter to bring the family along. For any gathering, there are many special arrangements that have to be made to ensure a successful event. If the invitation is for an adult function and little ones just pop in unannounced, their arrival is really not welcome. Not by the host/hostess, and not by the other adults at the event. Children require specific arrangements, and if they were not included on the invitation, then it is reasonable to say that these special arrangements have not been made.

When an invitation is received, formal, informal, professional, or casual, and you wish to bring a guest, always confirm with the inviter that your guest is welcome and expected. Never just show up with uninvited guests! It is rude, it is disrespectful, inconsiderate, and will most assuredly create a moment of embarrassment for you, for your uninvited guest, and for the host/hostess. A simple phone call or note to the inviter inquiring if it would be acceptable to bring an uninvited, special guest is a prior courtesy must—a courtesy that is strongly suggested by social and proper etiquette and will be appreciated by all concerned; a few minutes of your time that will prove once again, that to assume is not the path to take. One more note on this subject: if this person is not by commitment to the invited guest in an engagement or recent marriage, never assume that it is proper to just make a call. Also, self-invitation, even to a family gathering, is really not the path to take.

Chapter Nineteen

On a Date

DATING IS A subject that deserves an entire chapter all its own—a topic that is especially close to my heart as I have lived in a neighborhood filled with young people of dating age, and I have raised three children of my own. For these reasons, I can safely say that the sport of people watching on this most entertaining topic has been enjoyed by our family on a very regular basis. Whether standing in the living room of my own home and glancing out the window at the neighborhood, or taking a step back into time and enjoying a front-row seat as my own family members muddled through the awkward motions of dating. Either way, the stories never cease to amaze me—or any parent for that matter.

As the pages on dating unfold, I am confident in saying that the experiences we have all shared, either by chance standing on the sidelines or from a front-row seat by personal or family obligation, are all experiences that we can laugh and cry about and are all now shared in story form among friends and family alike.

It is a Saturday night and everyone is sitting around the dining room table, enjoying a relaxing meal with family or friends. From a distance they are all disturbed by the sounds of screeching tires squealing around the corner, then slamming to a sudden halt. Next, the echoing blast of a vehicle horn penetrates through the walls of the dining room and the guests are forced to brace themselves for the next explosion, watching the water in the glasses swish back and forth like the result of an elephant doing a belly flop in a swimming pool.

So much for a night of relaxation, as it soon becomes apparent that the reality of the sounds invading the once quiet neighborhood have just set the stage for the announcement that your precious daughter's boyfriend has arrived to pick up his date.

Oh my! What just happened? As a parent of dating-aged children, you do have the right to enforce a few simple courtesies that are expected from anyone as a vehicle is entering into your space, and when these courtesies are displayed, they play like the sweet songs of summer. Theses simple courtesies include no squealing of tires, no explosions, and no horns honking and no invasion of your quiet space.

A quiet, and somewhat controlled entrance into the neighborhood would be appreciated. No sound of rubber peeling around the corner that can only occur as the pedal hits the metal. And no sound of screeching brakes as the vehicle comes to an abrupt stop on the corner of your nicely manicured front lawn. Is that too much to ask?

Then, the sound of the vehicle door closing, firmly but properly—no slamming of a heavy door as the driver of the car actually approaches the family residence. And a gentle knock on the front door or the soft music of the doorbell ringing, sending the message that Date Man has arrived, would be nice. Comforting sounds that are so much more desirable than the annoying blasts of the car horn, which only holds second to the yelling out of a car window advising everyone within a five-mile radius that Date Man is waiting.

And last, but certainly not least, the reassuring sounds of a few simple words from the young man standing on the other side of the door, presenting himself properly, with a smile followed by a polite hello. A simple greeting offering a small nibble of security to the parents that even though the clothes may be a bit extreme and the half-inch peephole worn proudly as an earring may not say "Armani," the personal arrival at the front door, and the "hello-Mr.-and-Mrs.-Jones" greeting, certainly does imply that Date Man does have manners and somewhere along the way, these manners sunk into his memory bank and are now being presented, politely and with respect.

A short time ago, I was in my kitchen getting ready to start dinner, and out of the corner of my eye, there came the unforgettable sounds of squealing tires coming around the corner. As I looked up, I caught a glance of a brand new SUV ripping around the corner, speeding past my house. A middle-aged woman was sitting behind the steering wheel, and a young man, probably fifteen years old or so, was comfortably seated in the passenger seat beside her. The SUV stormed past my kitchen window, coming to a sudden stop at the top of the cul-de-sac, parking by the curbside, two wheels actually on the front lawn of the neighbor's yard. And you guessed it, this neighbor just happens to have a lovely young daughter who was apparently waiting on the front porch for her prince and carriage to arrive.

Yes, for that moment, I was guilty of stepping into the shoes of the nosey neighbor and did move directly in front of the kitchen window to absorb the reality of what had just happened and what was about to take place. And as my greatest fear unfolded before my eyes, the young man remained seated in the passenger seat of the SUV, extending not even the slightest effort to open the car door for his princess. And as the woman, who I guessed was the young man's mother, sat steadfast behind the steering wheel, and then laid on the horn with three consecutive blasts, the lovely young lady shot down the driveway like a pony coming out of a gate at a horse race. She bolted toward the waiting SUV, making the fifty-foot distance in less than five seconds. Then, in a split second, this lovely young lady opened the door by herself, leaped into the back seat, and then closed the door behind her. And like a blot of greased lightning, the SUV took off into the sunset, screeching around the corner. And the mom, talking nonstop over her shoulder to the passenger in the backseat, was oblivious to the reaction of the kids on the sidewalk and the glares of all of the neighbors peering through the windows. The SUV with the mom behind the wheel sped away as the young lady held on for dear life in the back seat. At the risk of sounding like the ring leader of the nosey neighborhood club, "What the heck just happened, and what was up with that mom?"

I have a question for you. Is this new method of picking up a passenger improper, rude, and possibly a bit on the lazy side? Oh yes! Not only is it improper, rude, and annoying to the people in the neighborhood to be forced to watch out for their lives as race car momma enters the cul-de-sac; it is also disrespectful to the person who is being picked up, not to mention the parents of this young lady, who are hanging onto the drapes in total fear for their daughter's life as they watch out the front window. In addition, it is a blatant display of reckless endangerment. Hey, race car mamma, have you ever heard the word *liability*?

As we really do not have control of the visitors in our neighborhood, we can only live in hope that someone, possibly the parents, would offer some instructions on a few safety rules, and maybe encourage the awareness of the speed limits in a residential area. Is that too much to ask? The speed limit question is on most driving tests.

I guess that some people really feel that the shrieking of tires and the blast of a car horn are a proper announcement for the pickup, but the question should be the announcement or pickup of what? Certainly not a friend or someone you care about. In fact, I don't think our pets or even our enemies would respond well to this type of pickup. To those who have been taught the basics of proper etiquette and simple grace, the blast of a horn seems to scream, "Hey, the carriage has arrived, so move your buns into high gear; I'm not waiting!"

What kind of an excuse is this for the arrival and pickup of a date? Quite frankly, I doubt that my daughter would have been permitted to bolt out the door toward a blasting horn, nor would she have been given permission to take part in this type of behavior displayed by an adult or parent. Wow, talk about the fear of becoming the product of your environment! And who needs to be around that kind of environment? The sad part of this story is that Date Man's mom obviously didn't have a clue.

Let's talk logistics here. The distance from the pickup vehicle to the front door of any house could never be that great. After driving into a neighborhood at the proper speed, slowly pull the vehicle alongside of the curb and stop. That wasn't difficult, was it? Then turn the key, which turns the engine off, get out of the vehicle, and make that journey to the front door. Upon arrival, bring your arm up just a hair and knock! Or take the more relaxed approach and use that little forefinger to push the doorbell. When the door opens, a simple hello is all that is expected. You don't have to recite the Gettysburg Address; just say hello. Not the work of a rocket scientist!

People, if you are picking up a date, believe me, taking a few minutes to walk up to the door and politely say hello to the parents or whoever answers the knock or doorbell will make a greater first impression than laying on the horn and expecting your date to run out to your vehicle as the family peers through the window, their minds filled with all kinds of fears and judgments.

And whatever happened to those precious words "Good evening" or "Hello, Mr. and Mrs.—?" We all have names so use them! A polite greeting and addressing a person with a title and name is the proper thing to do. Is simple grace and common courtesy really a thing of the past? I don't think so. As parents, we are not asking for a thirty-minute conversation or a game of twenty questions; just a simple hello as we look into your face—that is all that is requested.

Remember, first impressions will last forever! It only takes a few seconds to make that good first impression that will carry you through a lifetime. Making the effort by showing a few good manners can take you so much further than a loud and annoying blast of a vehicle horn honking from a distance. As a parent, the comfort of seeing our loved ones leave with someone who we can put a face to, rather than being forced to peer out the window at the outline of a body seated in a vehicle—who could very well be the axe murderer that was just on the news—could be ensured just by having someone make the journey to the door and say hello. A simple smile and polite greeting can place parents in a seat of comfort surrounded by a sense of relief that their daughter will be treated properly instead of throwing them in a room of fear—a room where the imaginations of Mom and Dad take over, along with the idea of introducing the family's weapon collection, which is placed neatly by the sharpshooter medal earned by Dad that says silently, "You, Date Man, have successfully made a bad first impression, and we are not in our comfort zone with you."

A smile and a few polite words are all it takes to ensure a warm welcome for that second date and can be achieved by taking a few extra minutes to walk to the door and say hello.

This practice is not restricted to one person arriving for pickup; it applies across the board. If a group of friends are getting together for an event, at least one person from the group should take the time to walk to the front door, greet the family, and then walk with the friend to the waiting vehicle. Again, remember that first great impression that will last for a lifetime will be made by speaking a few polite words and offering a sincere smile rather than the blast of a honking horn, or a scream from the car window as a car full of mysterious people wait in a parked vehicle far, far away.

On your next date, make it perfect from beginning to end by following a few easy suggestions, nothing difficult but suggestions that can certainly make the difference and will definitely be the steps to a great first impression.

We all love chocolate so look at the steps of building a good first impression as if they were brownies and start adding up the points. You start with a simple brownie and add different delightful toppings that build up until you create the ultimate brownie extravaganza!

When picking up your date or friend at their home, your foundation, or base to this extravaganza is The Brownie. Get out of the vehicle, walk to the door, and greet whoever opens the door with a polite hello. Addressing the person properly by title and name is like the caramel inside of the brownie, a smooth addition flowing toward that good first impression. If a gentlemen, dad, or brother is the greeter upon arrival, a handshake is the next step. I understand that in today's world, a handshake may be a bit foreign for some, so let me make it easy for you.

First: Extend your right hand toward the hand of the gentleman you are greeting. Good.

Next, shake his hand; a firm and limited shake is all that is required. Firm, but not a bear grip, as this is not the foundation of a wrestling hold. A limited shake, just a few seconds, is all it takes. Shaking and shaking and soon dislocating the arm of the father or brother of your date is probably not the best step toward impressing the family. And make sure that the handshake is a solid shake, not a limp wiggle. If you want to greet a lily leaf, walk out to the garden and say hello to a flower.

If a lady is the greeter upon arrival at the door, a simple and polite "hello" will do. Etiquette suggests that shaking the hand of a lady is not required unless the lady extends her hand toward you first. In fact, in some cultures, shaking the hand of a lady is a display of disrespect.

A handshake is usually a manly gesture. A firm but appropriate handshake offered as a step of an introduction to a greeting, solid and limited. No knuckle banging or high-fives, please.

If you have never met the family of your date, or some time has passed since you have been at the family home, it is always nice to introduce yourself. "Hello, my name is..." Again, a short and simple introduction is all that is required.

Alright, the greeting and introduction went well, so on to the next step. Perhaps it is a bit chilly outside, and a coat or wrap of some type is needed by your date. As a gentleman, it is time to make your next move toward making a good impression by assisting your date with her outerwear. The next step in the building of the brownie extravaganza, shall we say, is the scoop of ice cream.

Assisting with a coat or wrap is something that we don't see very often anymore. To a lady, when someone assists you with your coat or sweater, it is a true sign of a gentleman. This is a step in courtesy, or for now, the scoop of ice cream on top of the brownie, and will take only a few minutes of time but will leave an incredible impression, similar to the creamy, rich ice cream atop a hot brownie that just melts in your mouth.

To assist your date with her coat or sweater, first pick up the wrap, holding it at her shoulder height, and stand next to her. Hold the wrap comfortably so her arms can easily slip into the sleeves. If the wrap is being held too high or too low, this courtesy may ultimately become a battle. When your date has comfortably placed her arms into the waiting sleeves of the wrap or when the wrap is resting on her shoulders, step back. Now how easy was that? And it takes less time than scooping the ice cream on top of a brownie.

The next step in building the ultimate brownie extravaganza is the departure. Before you make your move to the waiting carriage, a simple verbal action acknowledging the greeting that has just taken place is a must—it is the fudge sauce.

You walked up to the door, announced your arrival by ringing the door bell or with a simple knock on the door, then offered a polite greeting, making eye contact with the family. You introduced yourself once again, simply and politely. Nice!

You assisted your date with her wrap and now it is time to depart—almost time. Before you make your move down the driveway toward the waiting carriage, you once again must make eye contact with the family members. Look directly into their eyes, and let them know in simple words that you enjoyed meeting the family of the person you have chosen to spend time with. Simple words like "It was very nice to meet you," would be a good beginning or if you have met in the past, perhaps "It was very nice to see you again," would be a proper choice of departure words, even though the meeting may have not been so nice as you were scared to death, shaking in your boots for the short time that seemed to be an eternity.

Just an FYI: This is not about you, Date Man; it is about the person you are picking up and her family, so remember the parental comfort zone—the fudge sauce that sweetens the deal—which if presented properly and politely, will make your next departure from the family door a sweet experience.

It is now time to make the long journey back to the waiting vehicle, knowing full well that all eyes are upon you. Keep the creation of the brownie going strong in your mind—this is the whipped cream. As a male, you take your position next to your date, moving at normal speed toward the waiting vehicle. Never walk in front of your date; you are not leading a horse back to the stables. Walking next to a lady is socially suggested in the Western world as ladies are always treated properly and equally. Walk normally; there is no need to run. This is not a race and running in front of your date, leaving her in the bushes, will not give you any sprinkles in the brownie-point department in your date's mind or the minds of the family watching through the window. Even when there are two or more guys or girls walking together toward the waiting vehicle, walk together and enjoy the journey.

Very nice! You have now arrived at the waiting carriage; what next? Here comes the maraschino cherry on top of the brownie. As a male, it is your duty to open the door. You wait for the female to board the vehicle, and then you close the door behind her. Wow, what a concept. You open the vehicle door, your date gets in the vehicle, and you close the door behind your date. If you are with a group of friends and you both are boarding the back seat of the vehicle, great! As a gentleman, you still open the door, let the lady board and take her seat first, then you board sitting next to the lady, closing the door behind both of you.

If a female is picking up a male friend, the rules of etiquette still apply. The lady gets out of the vehicle and walks up to the door. The lady will knock on the door or ring the doorbell. And when the knock or ring of the doorbell is answered, the lady will make eye contact and greet the person who has answered the door with a polite hello. As for the assistance with the wrap, gentlemen, you are on your own! After acknowledging the meeting with a few polite words, just like before, make your way to the waiting vehicle. No running; walk together as equals to the waiting vehicle. As a female, it is not your place to open or to close the door behind a male guest, but once again, it is up to the male to honor the door duties. Keep remembering the parental comfort zone and the building of that scrumptious brownie, by layering on the points—points that will soon become a daily practice in good manners. Now you may drive away into the sunset!

You have arrived at your destination and are getting out of the vehicle. So what do you do next? This should be an easy one, and here is the plan to follow if you are the gentleman.

First, you get out of the vehicle.

Second, open the door for the lady, assisting her if need be.

Then shut the door behind her.

If you both are in the backseat, you, as the gentleman, will get out first. Facing the backseat, and your guest, extend your hand to assist your guest out of the backseat. No pulling; your hand is extended as support, not a hoist. When she is comfortably out of the vehicle, close the door behind her. Bravo!

Let's look at a few types of dating scenarios. There are many types of dates that a couple can go on, but a few stand out from the rest. There are Party Dates, Dinner Dates, and Movie Dates. All of these are social gatherings, and proper etiquette must be adhered to using simple guidelines. So, you have picked up your date, and have arrived at your destination—what's next?

THE PARTY DATE

You are entering the party and the first action that will be taken will be the introductions. Oftentimes, although you may know everyone at a gathering, your guests may not. Take a few minutes to extend the courtesy of a simple introduction. As you walk into the event and approach the guests in this space, stop for just a moment and take the time to introduce the friend or friends that you are with.

A very simple "Hello, this is (and say the name)," followed by a handshake, a smile, or friendly hug is just perfect, and, yes, if knuckle banging is your thing, then bang away—as long as you are not banging on the hand of an adult. After you have spent a reasonable amount of time with this person, and when the timing is just right, move to the next person, making sure that an introduction is made each and every time you stop to say hello. If the guest, or guests you have brought with you are introduced to the host/hostess and surrounding guests in the space, that space becomes a comfort zone for everyone, ensuring that everyone will have the best time ever because they all will have someone to talk to.

Never assume that everyone knows everyone else; that rarely is the case. And always remember to introduce each person by name. If one can associate a name to a face, the door will open for a topic of conversation whether you are nearby or not: a common interest that keeps the party going that can make the difference between having a good time and standing in a corner like the party wallflower.

If you are the new guest on the block and you have accepted an invitation to a gathering and will be arriving alone, you may have to make your own introductions. This may be a little scary but it is not out of the question. Simply enter the space with a friendly smile, and begin circulating. You know, approach, meet, and greet. Standing in the corner, waiting for strangers to come to you, makes for a very lonely and unsuccessful party experience, and your silence may suggest that you are really not excited about being at the gathering because you have not shown any interest in the guests or the party surroundings or made any effort to meet anyone.

These simple suggestions apply to young and older guests alike. Oftentimes, being silent is mistaken for being rude. We have already covered that point. And if one does not at least put forth the effort by making a move or offering a simple introduction and a few nice words, chances of having a great time are about the same as being showered by thousands of diamonds. I would not suggest that you hold your breath on either account.

The wallflower at a gathering is noticed, but not often in the most complimentary light. It only takes a second to make an impression, and a good impression is much nicer to deal with all the way around.

Here is another situation. You and your lady have arrived at a party as a couple, and you are walking from room to room of the party space, side by side. The question here is which side of your lady should you, as the gentleman, be on? Old world etiquette says that the lady is on the left of the gentleman in most cases. The reason behind this etiquette rule is that in the days of kings, queens, and knights, the right hand of the man must always remain free to pull his sword in protection of those around him. So to have a lady positioned at a man's left is the "right" approach. Catchy, don't you agree? And of course, there are a few exceptions to this old world etiquette rule as well.

When walking down a sidewalk, the male should always walk on the outside or street side of the walkway, securing the female on the inside or building side of the walkway. You certainly don't want a team of wild horses to come up on the sidewalk and trample over your lady, do you? However, sometimes, the left of the gentleman can be the building side, depending on which direction you are walking. So rule of thumb is, when walking with your lady down a sidewalk, always remember that you, as the gentleman, will be on the street side.

When sitting at a table, the lady will be seated on the left of the gentleman. We have all been at a dinner party, awards dinner, or evening function and the place cards have been organized lady/gentleman around the table. Not only does this seating arrangement make for a more enjoyable mix of conversation, it is also very appealing to the eye—a perfect Kodak moment, so to speak, and is the proper seating arrangement.

The evening has come to an end; the party is over, and you are getting ready to leave. First, bid your farewells to the host/hostess of the event and the friends around you. If a male, offer and assist with a coat or sweater for your date. Walk side by side to the vehicle parked outside and open the vehicle door, boarding as before and you are on your way.

THE DINNER DATE

Of course there is more to dating than picking up and returning your date property and safely. And what a wonderful opportunity to review a couple of very important items discussed in prior chapters that also apply to dating. Many social events are associated around a meal, most often dinner, so let's talk about a *Dinner Date*. No one is saying that on each and every date based around dinner the attire should be formal and that it is necessary to take out a loan to pay for the meal. We all know that for most young people, both requirements would be impossible, not to mention ridiculous. A dinner date can be as simple as a picnic in the park or a hamburger at the local diner. I will stay with the example of the American teenager, though the rules do apply to all of us. A very common dinner date for this age group is a *pizza date*—taking a special friend or meeting up with a group of friends at the local pizza parlor and sharing a pepperoni pie and great conversation for a couple of hours together.

Even though the surroundings at a pizza parlor are very casual, proper behavior is still appreciated. Notice that the word, *appreciated* is used in lieu of the word *mandatory*. Why? Because even adults behave differently in a casual surrounding, but differently does not mean forgetting table manners or not extending common courtesies. There are a few suggestions to ensure that everyone has a good time even in a casual setting. Remember the comment made in earlier chapters that if one is given a paper plate and a plastic cup, the behavior is considerably more relaxed than if one is given a china plate and a crystal stem? True, so the next time you are able to experience both of these settings, step back and make a mental note, as there is a blatant difference in behavior and there should not be. Whether the meal is served on paper or china, the key here is that it is up to the individual to determine the appropriate behavior and perhaps one good rule to follow would be the consideration of those around you. I have orchestrated and hosted events in casual settings using both paper and china and have seen firsthand, appropriate and inappropriate behavior by young and old alike. Just because there is no worry about breaking the plate when using paper, that does not justify bad manners and inappropriate behavior. At a pizza parlor there are enough obstacles to conquer, such as the noise issue because the kitchen is usually open to the eating area. This kitchen/eating setup is becoming more and more common in many establishments, and the noise level from the kitchen encourages the volume level of the guests to be turned up like the new sound system in Dad's brand new sports car, whereas at a social event, such as a wedding or corporate dinner, the kitchen is in another space and the noise level is usually background music which is controlled. This is not by chance; it is prearranged and there is a good reason for it. When the music is presented in a soft and calm manner, yet can still be heard, the volume of the conversations are kept at a level only engaging the people at the table or on a one-to-one basis. If you really think about it, in most situations, the background music will be instrumentals rather than vocals during dinner. Musical selections performed soft, slow, and relaxing invite a lower sound level of conversation as no one feels the need to talk over anyone else—no competition between band and man!

While sitting at a dinner table, there is expected conversation in any meal setting and when the conversation is forced to compete with loud music, the words from the vocalist or the noise from the kitchen, the voices around the table increase in volume, resulting in a battle between the sounds. Referring to appreciated proper behavior exists for this very reason—although seated around a table at a pizza parlor, the loud surrounding sounds encouraging the guests that they must yell to be heard it is not acceptable. Surprisingly, not everyone feels that what you have to say is important, especially the elderly couple seated in the booth next to you.

Have you ever noticed that if the presentation of your words is projected in a calm and controlled manner, the people around you tend to lean in and listen, actually hearing what you have to say? But, if your words are barked out at a decimal level equal to a twelve-piece band, the words are muddled and lost among the surrounding noise and no one can hear what is being said. One conversation becomes lost among all of the conversations shouted back and forth across the table and the people seated at the tables around you are annoyed and are chiming in with loud requests to keep the volume down. Moral of this story, you as an individual are in control of the volume level of the conversation. If there is kitchen noise behind you, there is still no need to shout over that noise; your words will eventually become a mass of confusion and frustration. You may want to try leaning in toward your date and calmly sharing what you have to say. In turn, your date will appreciate your refusal to compete with the surrounding noise and will most likely feel that what you have to say is important and only for your date. This suggestion holds true for a group of friends as well—be in charge and in control of what you say and how your words are presented. Remember that you are still seated at a dining table and manners must still be considered. Your date will appreciate it, as well as the people around you.

When you walk in the door of any food establishment for a dinner date and are seated at the table, the same rules and guidelines regarding manners apply, whether it be a picnic table, in the center of a pizza parlor, or a finely dressed table in a formal setting.

YOU as an individual are responsible for your own actions.

YOU have your own meal space and your own napkin and your date or group around you have their own meal space and napkins.

And YOU know the proper use of the napkin and how to be seated and act while at a table and these rules do not change, *ever!* Even though pizza is one of the few main entrée foods that can be enjoyed with or without flatware, YOU as an individual must honor the rules outlined by proper and social etiquette when enjoying the meal. No one wishes to share the meal visually with you, so chewing with a closed mouth is a *must!* No one appreciates an uninvited fork in their plate and no one enjoys an elbow other than their own in their meal space. *Think about it,* after a date, do you wish to be remembered as the guy or girl who wore the pizza on his clothing and on his face instead of eating it? Or the date that ate the last piece of pizza even though it was on someone else's plate? I don't think so.

Remember the memory bank filled with basic etiquette and simple grace talked about throughout the pages of this book? The good manners learned along the way and all of these lessons stored in your own personal memory bank and the recorder going off and reminding you of what is proper and what is not? If the lessons that have been presented throughout this book, hand-in-hand with the lessons taught by your parents, mentors, and teachers, which have been stored in your memory bank, you can be assured that your own personal memory bank will be triggered; the lessons learned will be applied and your date will be a great success. In addition, the people seated around you at the pizza parlor will recognize and appreciate your manners. *How good you will feel!* And last, but certainly not least, I would like to make one more suggestion and it concerns the check presented at the end of the meal. If your date is someone you care about, someone you plan on seeing again, it would not hurt you to pick up the check. I completely understand that we are now in the twenty-first century and you do not have a money tree planted in your back yard, but a gentleman will still offer to take care of the meal and a lady will most definitely appreciate this cavalier gesture–*I guarantee it.*

THE MOVIE DATE

Another popular date is the *movie date* and this subject has been covered in a prior chapter, but it needs to be revisited once again, as we are still talking about dating. I can't count the number of times I have been standing in line to purchase a ticket for a blockbuster movie and gasped for air as I watched, in shock, the behavior of young people as the line grew longer—their loud voices booming, as if everyone around them really cared about what they were saying. Also the pushing and shoving, which is apparently a method of saying hello for some, but usually results in collisions with the other people standing in line. The less-than-appropriate attire leaving nothing to the imagination. And one mustn't forget the cutting in line, because for some strange reason, this young couple is under the impression that they are more important than anyone else and must enter the theater first. *OMG! Where IS Your Mother?*

I honestly cannot believe that this type of behavior is learned at home. But we are all products of our environment so if not at home, where? It seems to me that if proper behavior is required at a table, in a classroom, and in a house of worship, then it would also be required in any public place. Stand in line and enjoy talking to your date until it is your turn to purchase tickets–is that too much to ask? And again, if your date is someone you care about, purchase the tickets. It may be a good time to remind everyone that if you extend the invitation to dinner, a movie, or any paid social event, YOU pick up the check. That is considered good manners! When you and your date enter the theater, you may wish to stop by the snack bar, and again, if you extended the invitation, you purchase the goodies. And when you walk into the theater, you assist your date in any manner needed, then sit down and enjoy the movie. This IS the twenty-first century, so there will be no need to chime into the dialogue. The actors have been monetarily compensated very well for their performances and they really do not need assistance from you. Yelling at the screen is annoying to everyone seated around you, and besides, the actors cannot hear you! And when the movie has ended, wait for your date to gather her things and then walk together, side by side, and exit the theater in a respectable manner, continuing on your merry way. There are numerous gestures of good manners that should also be practiced while on a date, with kindness and consideration at the top of the list. In spite of what some may say, being considerate to those around you is the right thing to do; which is a perfect opportunity to once again share the old saying of "what goes around, comes around."

If kindness and consideration are shown to others, it will be received by you. There is never a good reason for bad manners, there is never a good excuse to be unkind or inconsiderate to others, and there is never a time or a place when being disrespectful to those around you is acceptable. From preschool through university, and even into relationships, both personal and professional, there are still those who feel that the way to get to the top is to be rude and cruelly assertive. Not true! The pit bull approach may be effective in a courtroom between battling attorneys, but in life, when dealing with family, friends, and business associates, pull in the fangs and extend kindness and consideration.

I would like to introduce an old expression from a previous generation that may hold true today and it is: "You can catch more flies with honey than with vinegar." Interesting and true, especially when you give it some thought.

Honey or vinegar?

As a child, you are playing in a schoolyard, and the new kid at the school is sitting all by herself wishing she could join the girls playing hopscotch. A little boy, all alone, is hanging out by the fence in hopes that he will be invited to play soccer with the boys.

This should be an easy one as well. Your honey/vinegar options as you notice the little girl sitting alone and the little boy standing by the fence are:

A. Invite the kids to join in and play (honey).

or

B. Ignore the kids watching and wishing (vinegar).

The correct answer of course is A, offer a little kindness and express consideration by inviting the kids to join in on the fun. This simple example can be applied in a similar manner at a party or gathering as an adult. No one wants to be the wallflower. Step up to the plate and make an introduction and the party is underway with an additional guest. Just another simple and suggestive tip that can be applied on the playground, at an adult function, as well as on a date.

We have now approaching the finishing touch of our brownie extravaganza. In review, picking up our date properly is the brownie. Addressing the person who answers the door in a polite and proper manner (and a simple introduction of yourself) is the caramel inside the brownie. Assisting your date with her wrap or coat is a creamy scoop of ice cream on top of the brownie. And a controlled and proper departure down the driveway is the cherry on top. Now, what's next?

The evening has come to an end; the party/dinner/movie is over, and you are getting ready to leave. Walk side by side to the vehicle parked outside and open the vehicle door, boarding as before. You are on your way.

And when you drive back into the neighborhood, show some respect to the neighbors by entering their space slowing—no racing. When you arrive at the house, stop the vehicle respectfully, and turn the engine off. Get out of the vehicle, offering assistance to your date, and then together, side by side, walk up to the door. This represents the sprinkles on top, the finishing touch to the brownie extravaganza!

It really is okay for a young person to be polite and courteous to a friend, a date, and the parents of the date. It is equally okay and appreciated by the neighbors if your entrance into and out of the neighborhood is done quietly and with some respect, especially at night. Being kind, considerate, and extending a sign of good manners can only make the date better—it really is okay. Okay and appreciated—I promise!

Chapter Twenty

Dressing for the Occasion

AT THE RISK of redundancy, let's be reminded that in life, there is a time for everything, and everything has its place. Dressing for the occasion certainly can benefit from this quote; however, any discussion on the topic of dressing for the occasion is a sure guarantee to be one that will fuel a very large fire. The same type of fire that we can also count on when discussing any form of politics, or belief, or practice of any religion. We all have an opinion on these hot and explosive subjects, but seldom can these opinions be discussed with friends, with family, or even with our spouse without starting a raging inferno. However, treading gently on the hot coals, I would like to give it a try.

Dressing for the occasion, any occasion, should be a simple and comfortable topic but for some reason, the words *simple* and *comfortable* usually do not apply. In today's world, due to the many styles and role models that this generation has to follow, the choices that are made can sometimes flip the lid off of a box labeled *appropriate* and can turn a delightful shopping spree with Mom into a war zone.

In addition, there are the groups that frown on any structured opinion in the matter of dress at all, proclaiming rights, prejudice, or lack thereof. What happened to the rules of etiquette making the subject of dress an easy and enjoyable subject to approach? And more importantly, good common sense—where did that go? There are no groups proclaiming the rights on these opinions or are there?

Only with kid gloves can the subject of dressing for the occasion be approached with suggestions from the etiquette experts of long ago, influenced by the many talented designers of today, and only encouraged by common sense can we begin to disrobe the fashion *faux pas* of today, in hopes of a somewhat more appropriate road to follow tomorrow.

When arriving at the office, walking into a classroom, shopping at the market, or stopping at a coffee shop for a morning cup of java, we witness styles and fashion statements worn by all shapes, sizes, and ages, and what we often see results in a less than desirable reaction—an experience in people watching that can bring a smile to our face or a tear to the eye.

In the world of event production, the opportunity to partake in the sport of people watching, with regard to fashion, opens the door to a front-row seat throughout the orchestration, continuing through the actual event. The experience of viewing the newest and hottest styles in attire and accessories worn as accents to the many fashion statements of today, by all shapes and sizes, in all walks of life, is as vivid as the bright lights on a Hollywood movie set, often offering an equally surprising story line.

For just a moment, you are all invited to take a step back in time, into the glamorous world of the 1950s, when fashion and the discussion of dressing for the occasion, any occasion, was as simple as picking up a magazine and flipping through the pages in admiration of two or three classic styles that were plastered over the pages; appropriate for all occasions and for all types of people in all walks of life.

You have just received an invitation to dinner with the Cleavers. You remember, The Beaver and Wally Cleaver? Mrs. Cleaver is in the kitchen preparing one of her family's favorite dishes, wearing a heavily starched and pressed white apron neatly tied around a tiny waist, masking a full skirted dress, in a bright floral print with the hem line resting just below the knee. The seam of her nylons traveling perfectly straight up the back of her calf and two-inch heels, known as pumps, with rounded closed toes in a sharp, yet traditional black leather completing her perfectly put together look. The final touch in the attire are the matching oven mitts worn on both hands, proudly holding a steaming baking dish of the family favorite, the crispy corn flake–topped tuna casserole. Yum!

In the '50s, we can all agree that the styles worn and accents added to complete any fashion statement were most appropriate for the home or for a trip to the market. As for the tuna casserole, well that may be a topic of further conversation.

The fact is, we are not living in the glamorous world of the '50s, so moving ahead to the twenty-first century, and once again, joining the Cleavers for dinner, probably at the home of Wally and Beaver Cleaver, just sit down and enjoy. First, with an invitation to dinner at a private home, guests would be considered company, so dress accordingly. No bunny slippers and no working-in-the-garden attire, no jeans with tears and big holes exposing the colorful foundation garments underneath. If the invitation is casual, a nice pair of slacks and open-collar shirt would be appropriate for the men, and pants and a sweater or a nice front-button blouse, fashionable top, or even a skirt would work for the ladies. Neat and complete would be the suggested look.

Have you all heard the saying "When in doubt, ask!"? A good statement that has been referred to in prior chapters and, once again, can be applied here. If there is ever a question of proper dressing for the occasion to a dinner invitation or any event for that matter, "When in doubt, ask!" If you are invited to a dinner, a party, a sports event, or any special event, and you are in doubt of what to wear, always ask! Ask the host/hostess, or another guest who will be attending what to wear, and the rest is up to you.

Fashion is a statement, and there are hundreds of styles that can make the statement. However, do you really want to make the wrong statement with the fashions you have selected? I don't think so.

Fact: It is not socially proper to wear casual denim, such as jeans, new or worn, to:

Most country clubs

An evening social event, such as a wedding

An awards event, business, or professional gathering

An opera, a concert, or a ballet

A prom or formal dance

Fact: It is not socially proper to bare skin, other than arms, the lower portion of the leg, and one's face at church, synagogues, or other houses of religious gathering. This social rule can be taken a step further as some churches or synagogues mandate that as a female, one's head and shoulders must be covered as a sign of respect. And in some religions and cultures, a woman's face must be covered at all times, also as a sign of respect and position.

At this time, it might be wise to apply yet another old saying with regard to choosing attire for any occasion, "leave a little something to the imagination."

Imagination is a form of excitement, intrigue, and even mystery; not only for you, but for everyone you come in contact with. Keep that little saying in mind the next time you are getting ready for any social event.

Fact: It is not socially proper to wear swimming attire into a restaurant or to school. This fashion fact should be an easy social rule to follow; however, take a moment and just look around. Where are the followers of this fact?

If you are on the beach and there is an outdoor eating establishment erected on the beach with picnic-style eating, some beach attire or swim wear may be acceptable, but never is it acceptable in a restaurant. Pay attention to the signs posted, respect the verbal requests of the establishment, use good common sense, and dress appropriately. If you read a sign that says, "we reserve the right of service" for any reason, you can be assured that if you enter an eating establishment dressed for all the world to see everything you have chosen not to cover, you will not be getting your burger and fries, or any other item on the menu for that matter. You will, however, probably be asked to leave, inviting lots of looks on your way out the door.

As for school attire, there should be no question as to how to dress for this occasion. Open the door on the old common sense memory bank and follow a few of the proper etiquette rules outlined by the experts followed by generations of long ago. When at school, the purpose of the experience is to learn, not to distract with inappropriate fashion choices. So please dress accordingly.

Fact: It is not socially proper to wear sleeping attire outside of one's own home, unless, of course, there is a slumber party, which one would dress in after arrival. The pajama tops or bottoms worn as shirts or pants to the market or to school are not fashion statements; it is a humungous fashion *faux pas*!

There are undergarments such as *camisoles* that can be worn under blouses or shirts, but the see-through fabric numbers with the less-than-single thread straps, should be saved for behind closed doors and not worn in the classroom, market, or on a lunch date—ever! As long as we are on the subject of appropriate dress for the classroom, here are a few social and proper etiquette suggestions.

Bare midriffs: No.

Bare feet: No.

Ratty and worn jeans that are resting parallel with the personal parts of your body that MUST be kept private: No.

Once again, when in doubt, ask!

Fact: It is not socially proper to wear flip-flops with anything other than swimwear or very casual attire. We are talking about the little rubber beach flip-flops; not the designer jeweled and beaded sandals with the strap between the toes that are worn during the summer months.

Flip-flops, the rubber ones, are for the beach, allowing one's feet protection that may be needed while walking through the sand. The little rubber flip-flops, offered in all colors of the rainbow, are not a fashionable shoe statement or substitute for a summer fashion for that matter. Flip-flops should be considered a quick fix for a fast trip across the hot sand just before taking a cooling dip, or jumping on a surf board and riding the waves.

The guiding factors in deciding what to wear to any event are directed by etiquette, common sense, and followed by fashion and fads. But there is a very important factor that is usually not considered when selecting personal attire and that factor is you! Yes, there are many selections, colors, styles, and fads to choose from, but are they for you? Do they fit and flatter your body type? Are they the most complimentary and appropriate color for your skin tone? Are they suitable for your personal and professional needs? When deciding on that perfect outfit for that special occasion, or even for that first day of school, take a few minutes and ask yourself these questions. If all of the answers are yes, you have made the proper selection in attire and will feel confident throughout the day. If any of the answers are no, revisit your closet. These questions also apply to hair styles, the application of makeup, and don't forget the fashions you select for your feet as they are also part of the attire—a total package that makes your own personal statement. So take a few minutes and get it right!

Making this proper attire thing a little easier for everyone, the proper dress for the proper occasion can be broken down into three separate categories:

Formal

Professional

Casual

Formal attire is most often black-tie (tuxedo) for the men and evening gowns (floor-length) for the ladies. Formal attire may be noted on the bottom of an invitation using the words, *formal attire, black-tie, black-tie optional,* and even *black-tie invited,* commonly seen in California, however, common knowledge in other states and countries. When an invitation is received with any of these four references to dress, then, gentlemen, it is time to visit a formal rental shop or shake off the mothballs from the tux that has been stuffed in storage, and for the ladies, let's go shopping!

Evening attire is less formal; however, if listed under the category of formal, evening attire is just what it says: attire suitable for an evening gathering. For men, a dark suit, slacks and coat matching in color, a collared, plain shirt buttoning down the front, and a nice tie to match. And for the ladies, a simple black cocktail dress, knee or tea-length, would be appropriate. There are other options, but it would be wise to remember those two little adjectives, *proper* and *appropriate,* and good taste will be the guide to the correct choice.

Professional attire is an obvious one and the word *professional* says it all. Professional attire applies to the office and continues through the classroom. If you work in a professional office environment, most often the dress will be outlined for you, quite possibly in book form, on a contract, or discussed verbally upon hiring. If not, professional attire is a more conservative form of dress. Some offices require a suit and tie for the men and skirts with jackets for the ladies. Other businesses may accept nice slacks with shirts or sweaters as their dress code. Again, when in doubt, ask!

Proper attire for school should also be a more conservative form of dress.

Alright, we all are aware that we are living in the twenty-first century, but that still suggests you should think conservative. You wouldn't wear a space suit to school and that is a fashion worn in the twenty-first century. The purpose of the classroom is a space to gather and to learn, correct? Inappropriate attire can be a distraction for whatever reason; how can one absorb any form of knowledge if there is a distraction? Denim jeans and a shirt; great! Linen pants and a top; ducky! T-shirts and walking shorts; works in California! When in doubt, just ask!

Remember that in an office, professional means professional, and at school, the attire must be suitable for a place to learn without distraction.

Casual attire can be shorts and shirts for the men at a pool party, or shorts and summer tops or a sundress for the ladies. Casual can also mean a nice jogging suit, pants and a shirt, or denim. Casual does not suggest sloppy or dirty. There is a big difference.

Any acceptable and proper statement in fashion can be directed by plain old common sense, so work on the list that works for you and share the list with your family, especially your parents and, if possible, your grandparents. If the statement in fashion you have selected is acceptable with them, sealed with the smile of approval, you are on the road to correct and properly dressing for the occasion. Dressing for any occasion will be a simple and comfortable task that you will be able to undertake every day and in every way.

Chapter Twenty-one

The Six O'clock Hat Rule

HERE IS AN issue that seems to scream fashion *faux pas*, and can be filed under the six o'clock in the evening candle rule in chapter fifteen of the book, but reversed. Social etiquette suggested by experts of the past say that a hat can be worn throughout the entire day up to six o'clock in the evening. That means that when the big hand on a clock reaches twelve and the little hand on the clock rests on six and it is evening, the hat is removed and placed in a safe place not to be worn again until the next day

Hats have always been known as a smart expression of fashion, and not so long ago, a hat was recognized as the finishing accessory to any fashion statement. Wearing hats seems to have fallen from the top step of the fashion ladder and they are not seen as frequently in the Western world as they were years ago. However, hats are still worn in other parts of the world on a regular basis and remain a very important accessory in any fashion statement for the well-dressed man or woman.

A fashion accessory is not a ball cap or a cowboy hat; however, it is suggested that they too should be removed after six o'clock when inside. If a hat is worn for warmth, or protection from the sun while outside, it is unusual for the hat to remain on one's head when inside—no sun and no wind or rain. With that said, the six o'clock rule is suggested by social etiquette and should apply to both men and woman, bad hair day or not. When entering a building or after six o'clock in the evening, the hat comes off! This rule was established many years ago in written form and was honored without question. Perhaps this suggested rule was based on good manners and common sense. I remember attending a university graduation that was held in the music hall on campus. It was a Sunday evening, and I was seated behind a lovely lady wearing the most beautiful, full-brimmed hat, and I could not see anything past the beauty of this hat. Not because I was focused on the hat, but because the hat filled the space in front of me. I then remembered the six o'clock hat rule that had been suggested by etiquette experts that I had studied and wondered if this lady had ever heard or read the rule.

So as suggested:

Do not wear a hat, any hat, in a restaurant. When you walk in the door, please take the hat off!

Do not wear a hat, any hat, at the dining table. I too love a ten-gallon Stetson cowboy hat and enjoy other fashionable headwear, but at the table, please take the hat off!

As a gentleman, do not wear a hat, any hat, when introduced to a lady. This is a proper etiquette rule that was established many years ago but the rule still applies. When a gentleman is in the presence of a lady, please take the hat off!

And as a gentleman, do not wear a hat, any hat, inside a building of any kind. This rule also comes into play when entering a church, a synagogue, an office building, or a movie theater. When you walk inside, please take the hat off!

Hats are wonderful and exciting fashion accessories that make a strong statement. Hats are to be worn with pride and in the proper manner that they were intended to be worn. I personally love hats: cowboy hats at the rodeo or fair, ball caps at a Dodgers game, a floppy rimmed beach hat to keep the sun out of my eyes, and designer-labeled fashion hats to finish off a smart outfit in a most sophisticated manner. But, when the clock strikes six o'clock in the evening, the hat comes off!

Chapter Twenty-two

When White isn't Right!

IN THE WORLD of etiquette, there are specific *dos* and *don'ts* on the subject of the color white and when it just isn't right. Beginning with a little history introduced in the early 1900s, it was said that the color white was worn by a bride to signify purity—an honored color reserved only for a bride. Now hold that thought! If white is worn only by a bride, in the world of proper etiquette, does that mean that white would be inappropriate for anyone other than the bride to wear at a wedding? Bravo, that is exactly what it means. At a wedding, white is for the bride and only the bride. I cannot count the number of times I have witnessed female guests at a wedding who have chosen white as the color for their attire. I am not referring to lovely light beige, warm champagne, a blush taupe, or even a creamy café color that may be the color selected for the mother of the bride or the lady attendants. I am talking about white! Very bright and very white and every time this poor choice of color has been seen on a guest by the bride, the tears begin to fall by the bucketfull! A little rule of thumb that may come in handy on this topic is when you are invited to a wedding, it is the bride's day and everything will be the bride's way including the honor of being the only person attending the occasion to wear white! Visit the many colors of the rainbow and pick another color, because the bride is the only person at a wedding who wears white, and for a guest, white just isn't right!

Another point of etiquette history that assisted in the foundation of this wedding custom is that after the wedding day, the women in the family would cut up the white bridal gown and with tender, loving hands would make christening gowns for the children yet to come, once again carrying on the symbolism of purity. Now, if this rule seems unreasonable or even somewhat ridiculous, visit the romantic side of the story and the fairytale will all come to life. White is reserved for the beautiful bride and then for the children to follow.

There is another old etiquette rule in the Western world that applies to when white isn't right, simply suggesting: white is never worn before Memorial Day and not after Labor Day.

Hard to believe that there are rules that say when and when not to wear a certain color. But there is a social rule regarding the color white. Rules suggested by social etiquette and directed by proper etiquette that, until the twentieth century, were followed to the letter. Memorial Day falls in the late part of May and Labor Day is usually the first week of September, so this etiquette rule says that white is only worn during the summer months. Not before the end of May, and only until the first part of September.

Think of the color white as summer: light and bright, just like the sun shining brightly in the sky and pure, like the waves on a warm beach.

We all know that to some people, etiquette rules, especially those that dictate what we can or cannot be worn, mean nothing, and there are always those people who will push the rules of etiquette whenever possible. People who will wear a pair of white cotton slacks in the middle of December, or a white pair of shoes on Valentine's Day are, as per this old rule of etiquette, really pushing the rule.

In the past decade, famous designers have created wonderful winter-white fashions, a light and inviting white that is compared in color to the glisten of a fresh snowfall on a mountain slope; designers creating magical clothing using wools and all types of winter fabrics and there are many takers, because it is another beautiful option to be added to the once mundane winter colors.

The rule regarding white clothing was established in the early 1900s; still honored by some and ignored by many, using the excuse that fashions in the color white would not be available if they were not socially correct. My reply to that excuse would be that cellophane would not be available if it were not socially correct, and we certainly don't see many people walking around in fashions made of cellophane in the summer or winter, do we? The excuse is lame and makes no sense. Personally, I really like the old rule. The anticipation of wearing a color that can only be worn for a few months during the entire year puts a completely different spin on the idea; something fun to look forward to and something different, bright, and fresh! But, as per modern etiquette, it is a personal choice and far be it for me to enforce the "when white just isn't right" rule; I am only the messenger. As I always say: When in doubt, return to the rules of long ago. Follow the "safe path" directed by proper and social etiquette, stamped with the etiquette seal of approval and good common sense!

Chapter Twenty-three

The Three Magical Phrases

WE HAVE ALL heard the expression, save the best for last. Well, that is exactly what the final pages of this book have done. The very best of basic etiquette and simple grace. A most important refresher course on a lesson in good manners, once again guided by proper etiquette and social grace, and directed by good common sense are words that should be a part of everyone's daily life and used every day without thought or encouragement.

There are three magical phrases that we all should be very familiar with, and hopefully these phrases were introduced to us all at a very early age and their use continued throughout our daily lives. These three phrases are to be used each day in a number of situations—three magical phrases, which will now be referred to as the *Three Magical Phrases of Good Manners*:

Please

Thank you

Excuse me

We all should be familiar with the *please* and *thank you* good manner rules; however, the third good manner rule, *excuse me*, although equally as important, is often totally forgotten. No matter how young or old you are, good manners are essential to a full and confident life. So, let's begin by taking a few steps back into the past and revisit magical phrase number one.

WHAT DO YOU SAY?

Please. We can all agree that *please pass the butter*, and not *give me the butter* is the correct answer to the question of what do you say when requesting that an item be passed to you. We also can agree that we all enjoy doing things for others, even simple things, like passing the butter, but we don't enjoy being ordered or demanded to do so. *Please*, such a simple word, used as the prelude to any request, can magically turn a chore into a pleasurable action. The word, *please* is very pleasant to the ear, don't you agree? *Give me the butter* is a demand or an order and most often when a request is barked out, the wheels of the request hit the brakes rather than coast along on a smooth and enjoyable ride. *Please clear the table* or *please take out the garbage* sound so much nicer than the shriek of a demand or the bark of an order. Requesting a task to be done, no matter how large or small, politely using the magic word, *please*, will ensure that the request is received with eagerness to complete the task rather than anger that the task was even ordered.

Have you all heard the very wise phrase, "it is not what you say, it is the way you say it"? This phrase makes a lot of sense, and if applied each time a request is made, the results will once again turn into magic—the same magic as the word *please*. The tone of one's voice and the presentation of any request, hand-in-hand with the word *please*, will work like honey gathered by bees rather than vinegar poured on an open sore; another one of those very wise phrases from past generations that we touched on earlier and should already be filed in your memory bank for daily use. There is never a reason to bark or demand a request and remember the tone of your voice, along with the simple magic word *please*. The combination will be your assurance that any request that is made will be honored with a smile. Try it; it really works.

THANK YOU

When a request is made and honored, the next step to follow, and the second magical phrase, will be *thank you*.

Thank you for honoring my request, thank you for doing the dishes, thank you for picking me up from school, and *thank you for passing the butter*. Two little magical words that are very easy to say and must always follow the completion of any request without fail. Whenever you need something done, even a little something, you usually ask for help, correct? You make a request to a person to do or assist you in a job. And when the job has been completed, this is your cue to take the next step by offering a simple and free expression of appreciation. Two magical words, spoken directly to the person who has honored your request. If this verbal gift is extended at the end of a job, the next time you need help, that person you call on will happily oblige because you took the time to extend a simple yet magical gift of appreciation by saying *thank you*. *Thank you for your help*, and *thank you for a job well-done*. Easy words to say and very much appreciated. Great, now let's move on.

Do You Say *Excuse Me?*

Of course. *Excuse me* is very easy to say, yet powerful, and the third on the list of the *Three magical phrases of good manners.* However, it is often completely forgotten. Words that can perhaps erase "the rude" off of one's face, or cut the edge off of an improper act or motion—words that should be used in many daily situations.

There is nothing more frustrating than hosting a meal for friends or family and at the end of the meal, watching everyone scatter from the table like ants at a picnic without saying a word. No thanks for the effort, no compliments on the wonderful meal, nothing! Oh, how wonderful it would be to hear these few simple magic words instead of watching in silence and realizing that in a blink of an eye, the meal that you spent hours to prepare is now over, and the appreciation left behind is nothing, not a word, *zippo*! Forgive me, I almost forgot the dirty dishes left on the table and the sink full of pots and pans that need to be washed and put away. And we can't forget the napkin dropped in the middle of the dinner plate or piled on the floor. How about the words, *thank you*? Number two on the list, of course, to be said first. *Thank you* for the meal followed by, *excuse me* from the table, the third of the *Three Magical Phrases of Good Manners. Excuse me* is all that is required and would be the proper thing to do. Think about this one for just one moment.

The meal is over and everyone leaves the table, vanishing into thin air. And the host/hostess, left sitting alone at the table, begins to wonder:

Where did everyone go?

Was there something wrong with the food?

Was it something I said?

A simple *excuse me from the table* would be just fine and would certainly erase any questions. Now how difficult would that be to say? And a few kind words or compliments on the meal would not be too much to ask either. But most importantly, taking a few minutes out of anyone's precious day to extend an expression of simple good manners would definitely make all the hard work and efforts put forth by the host/hostess worthwhile, even if the host/hostess is a parent or spouse.

Wait just a minute, not *IF* the host/hostess is a parent or spouse— *ESPECIALLY* if the host/hostess is a parent or spouse.

Here is another example and one that is somewhat awkward to approach. A natural body function escapes you at an inappropriate time and is shared with everyone around, and, once again, no words, nothing, just a veil of silence allowing everyone in the space to react in their own way. Where is the *excuse me*? Have we all reverted back to the prehistoric days of the caveman where saying absolutely nothing was probably acceptable, as the English language had not yet been conquered? Talk about perfect timing to ask the question of "Where IS your mother?"!

These inappropriate and rude things may just happen, not always planned, but if they do happen, don't assume that this behavior is okay or proper in any way. To just sit there and say absolutely nothing, acting as if you, the offender, were not responsible, is not the path to take, even though your performance in ignoring the crude and certainly rude situation could be Academy Award material. A simple *excuse me* can help to soften the shock and will at least present the allusion that a few good manners are rattling around in your brain even though your actions may toot or blast a different tune.

Moving on. You are sitting in the middle section at a movie theater and the person seated next to you is having popcorn. Hot, buttery popcorn. The intoxicating aroma of the lightly popped corn and the butter is affecting your brain, encouraging a purchase of a big bag for yourself. You stand up and begin the journey to the outside aisle, which just happens to mean crossing in front of the popcorn guy sitting next to you. As you make your move, sidestepping ever so carefully past Mr. Popcorn guy, you hit a big bump in the road. The bump is the size thirteen shoes on the feet of the popcorn guy sitting beside you. What do you do? Believe me, this is not the time to just stand there and say nothing. You have a mission to accomplish and there are people everywhere getting ready to voice very strong opinions about your blocking the movie screen in the middle of a blockbuster. Solution?

A simple *excuse me*, spoken in a sincere, quite voice would be the proper thing to do. However, this is usually not the approach that the screen blocker will take.

How many times have you seen a person accidentally step on someone's foot and say nothing, zip? Or run into someone and start to laugh hysterically? How about when a person crashes into another person then takes on the tough-guy attitude, spewing a few unkind words then walking away as if it didn't happen? Or, even better, if the person acts as if the encounter was the other person's fault.

Rude? Yes, the ultimate form of rude and often the basis for a chain reaction that triggers a big shove or one of those in-the-face screams, followed by a few not-so-appropriate words.

If you are responsible for scattering after dinner, sharing improper sounds, stepping on a foot that is not attached to your own leg, or physically running into someone at any time other than as an opponent during a full-contact sport, stop.

Look into the eyes of the person you have offended, verbally or physically, and say, "*Excuse me*," sincerely and politely! Then and only then, do you have permission to go on your merry way.

Simple and polite words, magical words, spoken sincerely and at the appropriate time, speak volumes in the world of good manners and the promotion of goodwill—simple and polite words that are deeply appreciated when heard. These verbal expressions should be taught as soon as a child begins to talk and encouraged day after day throughout a lifetime. Simple, yet magical words that, when learned, can be filed in your personal memory bank, and then each time an occasion pops up, the recorder in your mind will automatically turn on, allowing the pathway for these words to pass through your lips with confidence and sincerity, resulting in a presentation of good manners—good manners for all to hear.

Honestly, I cannot express in words how proud I was when my oldest son, at the conclusion of dinner at his home, placed his two-year-old daughter on the floor before him and asked, "What do you say when you are finished with your meal?" And this little princess, with long blonde ponytails and big amber eyes looking up at her daddy replied, "May I please be excused from the table?" Daddy then responded, "Yes, you may," and in two seconds, the precious little princess then whispered a soft "thank you" and was on her way. My little boy, who is now a man with a family of his own, had truly listened to the lessons he had been taught and learned so well from the constant encouragement that was instilled throughout his formative years. He was now applying those lessons of long ago to his precious children. A lesson on the importance of using the magic words, *please, excuse me,* and *thank you* in one clean sweep that he was now teaching to his children. Alright, this is a grandmother story, but when I watched this lesson exchanged between my son and his daughter, I took a very special journey back in time, and I felt like the main rooster in a hen house, chest filled with pride for the whole world to see. When my son looked over at me, I could see in his eyes that he too shared that same pride. He saw that his little princess was a good student of this lesson in good manners, a good student just like her daddy. "May I please..." were simple words that were magic to the ear, and filled my heart with pride. A simple lesson in good manners that was taught so many years ago will be carried on for many years to come.

Afterword

Throughout the pages of this book, I have shared many lessons on etiquette and manners, made numerous suggestions in a simple, and hopefully, non-intimidating manner, and I am confident that even though the lessons shared and the suggestions made were presented simply, some of you may still be offended with the rules outlined and a few of you may possibly be a bit on the defensive with the suggestions made. However, I am equally as confident that after reading this book, most of you will take away bits and pieces of helpful knowledge and understanding from these simple and suggestive lessons and will begin to apply the lessons to your daily lives. You will now be able to file the information learned in your memory bank and then pull the lessons out as they are needed, always remembering that the life we choose to live in this world can only be made more wonderful by applying the knowledge gained through lessons taught by reading books, shared by our family, friends, and teachers and by watching those around us. It is a day-by-day participation in the sport of people watching, the amusing human pastime that can be a lesson in itself as to how, or how not to act in personal and professional situations. It is the understanding that watching, listening, and most importantly learning, are the solutions to becoming a confident and complete person—a person who has the knowledge and application of etiquette, both social and proper, and a person aware of good manners and simple grace. Obviously a person that will never be asked that most embarrassing question: "Where IS your mother?"

About the Author

I have been an event producer for many years and am honored to be described as proper and professional, passionate and very detailed. I have written numerous articles for bridal magazines, directed many classes for adults and children, and have been the keynote speaker at many national conferences on the subject of my book and the importance of etiquette and simple grace. On occasion, I have also been told that I am somewhat of a stationery snob, strongly believing that stationery is the introduction to an entire event and should always be done properly—and yes, I am one of those people who is guilty of turning a piece of stationery over to admire the reverse side; sorry, impulse, I imagine. My presentation of suggestions and information is calm and controlled, and my execution is detailed with clear explanations throughout. If I were to be placed in a particular "category," it would most likely be "very knowledgeable on the subjects I present and proper to a 'T' the majority of the time."

I was given a very long and difficult Greek name at birth by my paternal grandmother and aunt; a name that was certainly a mouthful to say, but one that carried a significant meaning, *giver of life*, derived from the name Eve. It was presented proudly by the matriarch of our family, and is a title that was demanded by my grandmother, passed down to me, and respected by all who bore our last name. I am not from a silver-spoon family, quite the opposite. I was raised simply, yet comfortably, with the importance of good manners taught on a daily basis. The families of both of my parents sailed to the United States from Greece through Ellis Island in the early 1900s; family values, hand-in-hand with the strength and belief of a strong family unity, were equally important—to be honored, protected, and respected at all times. The reception of family was at the top of the list with no reference to the clothes that were worn, or the jobs that were obtained, but that both, no matter how minimal, would be presented and performed with pride. Reception was the symbol of proper manners that were always displayed and simple grace was always present, which would be received by others at any given time. Family values seem to have been forgotten in the busy world of today; important values that many feel are the foundation of who we are and the ground level of our great nation—values that were and still remain the basis of our family.

Beginning at a very young age, I read almost every etiquette book in print, starting with Emily Post's *The Blue Book of Social Usage*, published in 1922, and continuing through the books written by her daughter, Elizabeth Post, and later by her granddaughter, Peggy Post. *The Amy Vanderbilt Complete Book of Etiquette*, published in 1952, was another favorite of mine, as well as numerous books written by Miss Manners and others. I absorbed the guidelines and views of each of the expert authors and now refer to their expertise in the writing of *Where IS Your Mother?*, and in lectures and seminars that I present. Through many years of personal and professional relationships, I've often referred back to the basics, those fifteen-hundred-page etiquette books that now sit on the shelf in anticipation of someone discovering their knowledge. I am frequently contacted by friends, family, associates, and even strangers referred to me by fellow associates with questions on basic etiquette and the proper actions of simple grace. Often the answers are quick to come to my mind as I reflect on common sense or what etiquette experts would say are the *Golden Etiquette Rules*, and I can safely say, without hesitation or any reservation, that my answers are the same answers that were probably given by my ancestors as they made their journey across the sea. The *Golden Etiquette Rules* that were established by the long ago experts, such as Post and Vanderbilt, will forever be proper and correct in our future; the same rules that simply remind us that when in doubt, return to the guidelines of old-world etiquette.

Today's world seems bereft of social grace and manners. There are no fail-safe manuals, or guides that can even scratch the surface of the basics of proper etiquette and simple grace. There are many how-to guides on raising our children, planning parties, or holding group gatherings; wonderful books, in coffee-table form, a number that are quite sensational in design and style, however, few with any mention at all of etiquette or manners. The simple basics of proper etiquette, of good manners, and of social grace, whether in a backyard enjoying a barbeque, in the school cafeteria, at a restaurant, or at home, remain the same.

Simple and proper values, presented with grace should be a part of our lives; especially in the world today, these values must be revisited and their importance reinforced, every day and in every way.